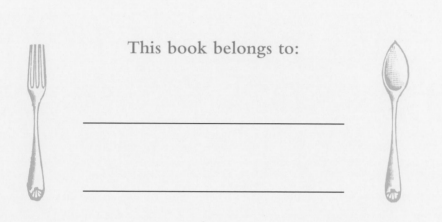

This book belongs to:

_____

_____

Gisela Allkemper

# Tomatoes
## Favorite Recipes

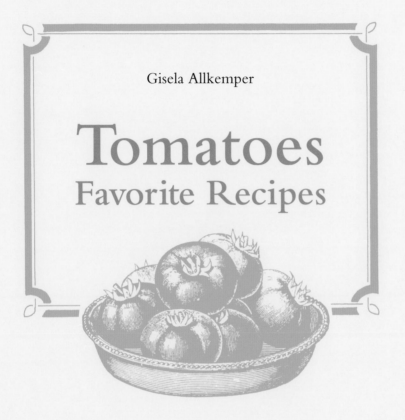

Published originally under the title Lieblingsrezepte mit Tomaten
© 2004 Verlag W. Hölker GmbH, Münster. English translation
for the U.S. market ©2005 Silverback Books, Inc.

Design: Niels Bonnemeier
Production: Patty Holden
Translator: Christie Tam
Project Editor: Lisa M. Tooker
Editors: Christiane Leesker, Ann Beman

ISBN: 1-59637-016-5

Printed in China

# CONTENTS

Unless otherwise indicated, all recipes make four servings.

# PREFACE

When Columbus discovered America and first established the link between the Old and New Worlds—and their cuisines—he never could have imagined that the tomato would make such a conquest.

Originally from tropical Central and South America, tomatoes are now available almost everywhere. More than 2,000 years ago, small tomatoes (called tomatle, or "swelling fruit") grew wild along the Peruvian coast. It was not until many years later that they were cultivated by the Aztecs in what is now present-day Mexico. Columbus first brought them to Europe when he returned from his second voyage to America in 1498. But at first, Europeans regarded them only as ornamental plants. They were extremely skeptical of the tomato's culinary value and even looked down on it. They believed the fruit was poisonous and made people "mad with love." That's probably how it got its other name, "love apple." It wasn't until 1820 that tomatoes began to be used—with some reservations—in salads and vegetable dishes. In 1840, to counter all the false information about the poisonous nature of this fruit, Colonel Robert G. Johnson stood on the courthouse steps in Salem, New Jersey, and ate a raw tomato, while onlookers cried out in horror. In Germany, the fruit went all but unnoticed until 1890. Today, tomatoes are extraordinarily popular and an integral part of any menu, both in summer and winter.

In this book, I present you with a selection gleaned from a large number of international recipes. Tomatoes may not always be the main ingredient, but they do give each dish that "certain something." I hope this book will be a valuable aid for cooking tomatoes so that you can say, like the late, great Julia Child, some more of this, a little more of that, "and voilà! The sauce is done." In this spirit, I wish you much success, bon appétit, and lots of fun cooking with tomatoes!

*Gisela Allzermper*

# THE TOMATO

## The Name

The Latin name for the tomato (Aztec name: Tomatle; from tomane = swell, thus "swelling fruit") is *Lycopersicon esculentum* or *Lypopersicum*, which basically means "edible wolf peach." The common name differs from country to country. In Austria, they're known as Paradiesapfel or Paradeiser (apple of paradise). In France they're called pomme d'amour (apple of love), but also tomate, as they are in Spain. In Greece, they are domato, in Italy pomodoro (golden apple), in the Netherlands Tomaat, and in English-speaking countries tomato or love apple.

## Nutritional Values

Tomatoes ripened outdoors in the sun are more nutritious than tomatoes grown in greenhouses or by hydroponics. The fully ripened fruit contains lots of ascorbic acid (vitamin C), malic acid, oxalic acid, sugar, and carotene. It is rich in trace elements, tannins, and minerals, plus 13 vitamins that make it a fountain of health.

Tomatoes also contain histamine and solanine. Histamine can cause allergies, and solanine irritates mucus membranes. It has been possible to remove all solanine from tomatoes through cultivation, although solanine may still be present in the cores and leaves, so caution is advised.

## Medicinal Properties

Tomatoes stimulate the appetite, act as a laxative and diuretic, and serve to detoxify the body. They protect the heart, circulatory system, and immune system, stimulate the stomach, intestines and liver, and prevent premature aging of the mind and body. The red pigment lycopene, found primarily in the peel, reduces the risk of cancer and prevents heart attacks and strokes. Combined with fat, it provides valuable provitamin A. Freshly squeezed juice has fewer calories than fruit juice and is also filling, making it suitable as an appetite suppressant. Tomato juice mixed with glycerine can also be used as a facial cleanser!

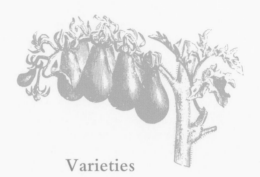

## Varieties

New strains constantly being developed now provide us with a wide range of colored varieties, including red, yellow, green, and even black. They also differ in aroma and cell structure. The following tomatoes are the most popular and most often used:

- Garden tomatoes: These are smooth, round, and red, are comparatively high in fruit acids and have a relatively large number of seeds. They're suitable for salads, as a side dish, or simply as a topping on bread.
- Vine tomatoes: Generally smaller, more flavorful, and sweeter than garden tomatoes with fewer seeds. They are also excellent in salads.
- Vine cherry tomatoes: Also known simply as cherry tomatoes. They're available in red and yellow and are sweet and extremely aromatic. You can eat them plain or prepared in salads and roasted dishes, or use them to decorate salads and cold platters.
- Beefsteak tomatoes: As the name indicates, these are meatier than the others, contain fewer seeds, and are less juicy. They're generally used for cooking but are also good stuffed.
- Oxheart tomatoes: These large, ribbed tomatoes take their name from their shape. They are prepared and used in salads, soups, and sauces.
- Plum or roma tomatoes: These elongated tomatoes have a very flavorful, sweet flesh. They taste great raw but because of their firmness, are also a favorite for pizza toppings and in casseroles.
- Green tomatoes: This can refer either to a green variety or to unripe garden tomatoes. Unlike those cultivated as green, the unripe kind cannot be eaten raw but are excellent for cooking and baking.
- Tomatillos: Mexican ground cherries, similar to tomatoes. The peel is brownish, inedible, and must be removed. The flesh is firmer than a typical tomato. Tomatillos are a standard ingredient in Mexican dishes.

# Cultivation

Originally from Peru and Mexico, tomatoes are now grown in all warm countries. Tomatoes love light and lots of warmth, so it's no wonder that the most important tomato-growing regions in Europe are around the Mediterranean. They also thrive in the warmer zones in America and on the Canary Islands. On Guernsey, an island pampered by the Gulf Stream, there is a tomato museum where you can glean a great deal of interesting information. One of the island's coins even bears an image of a tomato plant.

Like potatoes, tomatoes belong to the nightshade family. The plant can grow to a maximum height of 5 feet and has feathered leaves. Tomato plants require well-worked soil rich in nutrients, a sunny, protected location, and lots of water. Because the plants are frost-sensitive, they should first be sown in a greenhouse in February/March and not transplanted to the outdoors until at least mid-May. When the seedlings are 3- to 4-inches high, they're ready to be transplanted (separated). Transplant them to small pots (yogurt containers with a hole in the bottom will work just as well). This will allow them to develop sturdier stalks. Then plant them outdoors, leaving 31½ inches in between, and tie them to stakes. Trim the "suckers" growing out at the base of the leaves. Keep the soil moist but protect the tomatoes from rain, as they spoil quickly. Because tomatoes rapidly deplete the soil, be sure to fertilize the plants from time to time. Repeated applications of copper sprays protect against fungal diseases (such as tomato blight). Never plant tomatoes together with fennel. They don't tolerate one another and your tomatoes will be practically tasteless. The important thing is to let the tomatoes ripen fully on the vine! In September, you need to trim the growing tips at the top. This will accelerate the ripening process, which starts to slow down toward the end of summer. Let the last (including unripe) tomatoes ripen in a warm, lighted place. You can also extend the harvest time into the fall by hanging the entire stalks, with the tomatoes attached, upside-down and in a draft.

If you don't have a garden but do have a sunny, warm balcony, place the plants in large, wide pails. They'll do well like this, too. Mix peat into the soil. If you experience long periods of bad weather, protect the pails from the rain.

## Storage

- If possible, keep ripe tomatoes cool but do not refrigerate.
- Unripe tomatoes can be ripened in a warm, sunny spot in 2–3 days. To speed up the process, store them with apples or oranges.
- Do not store tomatoes together with vegetables such as cauliflower, cucumbers, or zucchini. They give off ethylene (ripening gas) that will cause the vegetables to wilt and soften.
- Canned tomato paste keeps longer if you transfer it to a glass or ceramic bowl and add enough olive oil to cover the surface.

## Processing

- A tomato is ripe if its surface is firm but yields slightly to pressure.
- Select the correct variety for your particular dish, because all tomatoes are not alike (see page 10, "Varieties").
- When processing tomatoes for raw consumption don't peel them; many nutritious vitamins are found in and just below the skin.
- When processing tomatoes for raw consumption, be sure to rinse them well beforehand.
- To slice a tomato, first use a sharp knife to remove the core by cutting it out in the shape of a wedge. Then use a tomato knife (with a serrated edge) to slice the tomato across the seed chambers, which will help keep the seeds from detaching around the flesh.
- If you're going to cook with tomatoes, you should first remove the peels. Otherwise the peels come off during cooking and interfere with the texture of the dish.

- Removing the peel: Cut an X through the skin on the stem end of the tomatoes and submerge for several seconds in hot water that is no longer boiling. Then dip briefly in cold water. You can now easily pull of the peels.
- Hollowing out tomatoes: Do not peel them. Cut a cap off the top. Carefully spoon out the flesh, seeds, and juice. Place the tomatoes on paper towels with the cut side down until ready to fill. You can use the interiors of the tomatoes for another recipe or freeze them unseasoned.
- To give bland tomatoes some flavor, add a little sugar or honey.
- Acidify salad dressings with only a dash of lemon juice or very mild balsamic vinegar. Vinegar destroys the tomato's natural acidity.
- You can enrich cooked tomato dishes by adding tomato paste.
- If you're inundated with tomatoes from your garden in the summer, peel and freeze them either whole, chopped, or puréed, but unseasoned. When thawed, they will be suitable only for cooking.
- Naturally, you can also preserve tomatoes. For more information refer to the section titled "Provisions from the Freezer & Cellar" on page 103.
- Canned tomatoes are an alternative in winter. They're available whole and peeled, chopped, puréed, or in the form of juice. Note that canned foods are richer in content than fresh. The same applies to dried tomatoes.
- In addition to salt and pepper, tomatoes are traditionally seasoned with herbs. Always add basil, chives, and chervil to dishes at the very end; you don't want them cooked. Thyme, oregano, sage, and tarragon, however, can be cooked.

# APPETIZERS & SNACKS

## Tomato Butter

*7 tbs dried tomatoes in oil (about 3½ oz), 3 anchovies,*
*7 tbs softened butter (about 3½ oz), 2 tbs ricotta cheese,*
*2 tbs dill tips, Freshly ground pepper, Several dashes lemon juice*

Drain dried tomatoes on paper towels. Soak anchovies in water for at least 15 minutes, rinse, and pat dry. Chop tomatoes and anchovies very finely. Knead together butter and ricotta. Mix in tomatoes, anchovies, dill, pepper and lemon juice, and mash with a fork. Refrigerate. Spread tomato butter on freshly toasted bread that is still warm. Delicious!

## Tomato Cheese Spread

*7 oz cream cheese (or spreadable feta cheese), 7 tbs crème fraîche\* (about 3½ oz),*
*3½ tbs butter, 1 tsp tomato paste, ½ tsp mustard, 2 plum tomatoes,*
*1 green onion or small onion, ¼ green bell pepper, Salt, Sugar,*
*Paprika, 1 tsp lemon juice, 1 tsp grated untreated lemon peel,*
*1 tbs finely chopped basil, ½ tbs powdered white gelatin (optional)*

Combine cream cheese or feta, crème fraîche, butter, tomato paste and mustard, and stir until creamy. Blanch tomatoes, peel, and remove cores and seeds. Clean green onion or peel onion and chop coarsely. Clean bell pepper and remove stem, seeds, and interiors. Chop tomatoes, onion, and pepper in a food processor. Combine with cheese and season with salt, sugar, paprika, lemon juice, lemon peel, and basil. If the spread is too runny, dissolve the gelatin according to package instructions and stir it into the mixture. Refrigerate. Keeps in the refrigerator for 2 to 3 days.

\* Crème fraîche is available in gourmet shops, or can be made by combining 1 cup whipping cream with 2 tbs buttermilk in a covered glass container at room temperature, about 70°F. Let stand for 8 to 24 hours, or until very thick.

## Melted Tomatoes on French Toast

Melted tomatoes are a delicious condiment for steak, meatballs, fish fillets, or omelets. Make sure the tomatoes are soft but not yet disintegrating. If necessary, you can shorten the braising time by placing them in the oven.

*4 large beefsteak tomatoes, 1 large onion, 1 clove garlic,*
*3 tbs butter, Dried herbes de Provence (optional),*
*2 eggs, Salt, 4 slices white bread, Freshly ground pepper*

Blanch tomatoes, peel, cut into quarters, and remove seeds and cores. Peel onion and garlic and dice finely. In a pan, heat half the butter and briefly brown diced onion and garlic. Transfer pan contents to a shallow baking dish. Arrange tomato quarters side by side on top. If desired, sprinkle with herbes de Provence. In an oven preheated to 250°F, cook (melt) for about 40 minutes.

In the meantime, beat eggs with a little salt. Dredge bread slices in eggs on both sides. Heat remaining butter in a pan and fry bread on both sides until golden-brown. Remove cooked tomatoes from the dish and distribute on the toast. Season with salt and pepper. Serve warm.

You can vary the toast as desired by also topping it with shrimp, bacon, or other goodies.

## Crostini

*12 slices baguette, Olive oil for drizzling, Salt, Freshly ground pepper,*
*1 cup beefsteak tomatoes, 7 oz mozzarella, 8 pitted black olives,*
*½ bunch oregano, 1 tbs cold-pressed olive oil*

Preheat oven to 350°F. Drizzle oil onto baguette slices, sprinkle with a little salt and pepper, and prebake in the over for 5 minutes. In the meantime, blanch tomatoes, peel, and remove cores. Slice tomatoes and mozzarella. Cut olives into rings. Rinse oregano, pat dry, pull apart into slightly smaller pieces, and dip in oil (to help it retain its color and flavor). Remove warm bread slices from the oven and top with tomatoes, mozzarella, olives, and a little oregano. Place on a baking sheet and bake in the oven for another 5–7 minutes. Remove, let cool slightly, and serve.

## Bruschetta al Pomodoro

Bruschetta (pronounced "brusketta") are a favorite snack in Italy, enjoyed after shopping or any time, and shared with guests.

*1⅓ cups sweet, fruity tomatoes (about 10½ oz),*
*1 handful fresh basil leaves, 1 clove garlic,*
*4 slices ciabatta or French country bread,*
*4–6 tbs cold-pressed olive oil, Salt, Freshly ground pepper*

Blanch tomatoes, peel, remove cores and seeds, and dice flesh finely. Rinse basil, pat dry, and cut leaves into strips. Peel garlic and cut in half. Toast bread slices and arrange on a platter, rub with garlic, and drizzle with olive oil. Top bread with chopped tomatoes and basil and season with salt and pepper. Serve immediately!

🍅 If you have too much chopped tomato, crumble in feta, spoon the mixture onto steak, fish fillets or sandwiches, and brown in the oven.

🍅 Sprinkle tomato bruschetta with grated Parmesan or lay anchovies crosswise on top.

# Jellied Tomatoes

*3½ tbs dried tomatoes, ½ cup red wine,*
*1½ cups consommé (recipe on page 31), Several dashes Tabasco sauce,*
*1½ tbs powdered red or white gelatin, 2 hard-boiled eggs,*
*3½ oz shrimp, 1 tbs green peppercorns, 2 tbs chopped chervil,*
*2 tbs chopped chives, Grease for the individual molds (optional),*
*Lettuce leaves and tomatoes for garnish*

Dice dried tomatoes and soak in red wine for 1 hour. Season consommé liberally with Tabasco. Stir in red wine and dried tomatoes. Soak gelatin according to package instructions, then melt over low heat, and beat into the soup. Refrigerate.

Chop egg whites (use egg yolks in another dish) and combine with shrimp, pepper, and herbs. Grease small molds or line with plastic wrap. When the soup starts to set, pour enough into each mold to cover the bottom. Let the gelatin become a little firmer and top with a layer of egg–shrimp mixture. Then pour in more soup and refrigerate again. Repeat the process until the molds are full to the top, ending with a layer of gelatin. Let set completely, reverse out of the molds, and garnish with lettuce, tomatoes, and, if desired, crumbled egg yolk.

# Tomato Mousse

*1 tbs powdered white gelatin, 2 large beefsteak tomatoes,*
*Salt, Lemon pepper, Celery salt, 2 eggs, 2 tbs heavy cream,*
*1 tbs chopped mint leaves (or 1 tbs green peppercorns),*
*Oil for individual molds or bowls, Smoked ham,*
*1 hard-boiled egg, sliced, Several small lettuce leaves*

Stir gelatin into a little cold water and let stand for 10 minutes. Blanch tomatoes, peel, and remove cores and seeds, saving any juice. Purée tomato flesh and juice. Measure out 1½ cups purée. If the tomatoes did not yield this much, supplement with orange juice, defatted stock, or red wine. Season liberally to taste with salt, lemon pepper, and celery salt. Separate eggs. Combine egg yolks, cream, and a little tomato purée and beat over a hot double boiler until smooth, but be careful—the mixture must not boil! Remove from heat and pour cream into remaining purée while beating vigorously.

Dissolve gelatin over low heat according to package instructions, stir into cream, and refrigerate. When the mixture starts to set, beat egg whites until stiff. Carefully fold mint leaves or green peppercorns into cream and season. Pour into greased, individual molds or glass bowls, and let gel completely. Reverse onto plates or scoop out balls with an ice cream scoop. Garnish with smoked ham, sliced egg, and lettuce leaves.

Variation: To add more flavor to the mousse, stir in 1–2 tsp tomato paste.

🍅 Spread a thick layer of mousse onto bread. Top with shrimp or toasted, chopped almonds. This is also delicious with trout caviar.

🍅 Serve tomato mousse with a yogurt-lemon sauce or in a pool of sauce.

## Avocado Tomato Cocktail

*1 ripe avocado, 1 tsp lemon juice, 2–3 tomatoes, 1–2 onions,*
*1 tsp salt, 2 tbs red wine vinegar, 3 tbs cold-pressed olive oil,*
*Chopped parsley or cilantro, Lettuce leaves for garnish*

Cut avocado in half lengthwise. Remove pit and peel. Dice flesh and immediately drizzle with lemon juice so it doesn't discolor. Blanch tomatoes, peel, remove cores and seeds, and dice flesh. Peel and grate onions. Combine 2 tbs grated onion (use the rest in another dish) with salt and add to diced avocado.

Combine vinegar, oil, and parsley or cilantro to make a vinaigrette and pour over the avocado-onion mixture. Line champagne saucers with lettuce leaves and spoon in mixture. Serve cocktail immediately as an "amuse-bouche."

## Tomatoes in Herb Cream

*3⅓ cups ripe, firm cherry tomatoes or small vine tomatoes,*
*1 onion, 1 clove garlic, 1½ tbs butter, 2 cups heavy cream,*
*1–2 tbs fresh chopped herbs (e.g., thyme, oregano, rosemary, Italian parsley,*
*chives, possibly dill tips; may substitute 2 tbs dried herbes de Provence),*
*Salt, Freshly ground white pepper*

Blanch tomatoes, peel, and remove cores. Peel onion and garlic and mince. In a saucepan, melt butter and lightly sweat onion and garlic. Pour in cream (also add dried herbs now). Simmer over low heat until the cream has been reduced by half. Stir in fresh herbs. Bring to a boil and add tomatoes. Season and heat briefly. The tomatoes should not disintegrate. Serve in pasta bowls with toasted bread or small party rolls.

Tomatoes in herb cream are an ideal appetizer but are also good as a side dish with lamb.

## Large Antipasti Plate

*For the vegetables: 2 small eggplants, 2 small zucchinis, Salt,*
*4 large vine tomatoes, A little flour, 3 tbs olive oil for frying,*
*16 slices feta or mozzarella, 16 drained anchovy fillets, Several pitted olives*
*For the dressing: 1 clove garlic, 1 green onion, ½ bunch basil,*
*2 tbs cold-pressed olive oil, 2 tbs lemon juice, 1 tbs tomato paste,*
*Salt, 1 tbs crushed multicolored peppercorns*

For the vegetables: Clean eggplant and zucchini and cut crosswise into slices
½-inch thick. Arrange slices side by side in a shallow baking sheet, sprinkle with
salt, and draw out water for 10 minutes. Blanch tomatoes, peel, remove cores, cut
into quarters, and remove seeds. Arrange tomato quarters side by side on a baking
sheet and dry in an oven preheated to 250°F for 30 minutes (leave oven door cracked open). Pat eggplant and zucchini slices dry and dredge in flour. In a large pan,
heat olive oil and sauté vegetable slices on both sides. On a large platter, alternate
eggplant, zucchini, and tomatoes in an overlapping pattern. Also top each tomato
quarter with 1 slice cheese and lay anchovies crosswise on top. You can also arrange
cheese and anchovies next to the vegetables. Sprinkle olives in between.

For the dressing: Peel garlic and clean green onion. Chop garlic and cut onion into
rings. Rinse basil, pat dry, remove leaves from stems, and cut into strips. Combine
olive oil, lemon juice, tomato paste and 2 tbs water, and season with salt and pepper.
Mix in garlic, onion and basil, and drizzle spoonfuls of dressing over the antipasti.

🍅 You can also sprinkle grated Parmesan onto the zucchini and eggplant.

## Stuffed Tomatoes

Whether cold or oven-browned, stuffed tomatoes are always welcome as an appetizer or light snack.

Preparation: Cut a cap off of uniform-sized beefsteak tomatoes (as an appetizer, 1 per person is enough) and set aside. Remove interiors of tomatoes using a sharp knife. Spoon out seeds and juice (use juice for another dish), being careful not to pierce the sides or bottom. Set tomatoes upside-down on paper towels to drain. Prepare fillings according to the recipe (see pages 22–24), spoon into tomatoes, and bake. As cold fillings, you can use salads that go with tomatoes and ingredients that are finely diced or grated (a classic example is egg salad).

## Scrambled Egg Filling

*Per beefsteak tomato: 1 small egg, 1 tbs heavy cream,*
*Salt, Freshly ground pepper, ½ tsp chopped parsley,*
*1 tsp diced bacon, 1 tsp diced onion, Grated cheese, 1½ tbs butter*

Whisk together egg, cream, salt, pepper, and parsley. In a nonstick pan, briefly brown diced ham and onion, let cool, and stir into egg. Pour mixture into prepared tomatoes. Sprinkle with grated cheese and replace cap on tomato.

Grease a casserole dish with a little butter and arrange tomatoes inside. Cut remaining butter into bits and distribute over tomatoes. Bake in an oven preheated to 425°F for 15 minutes.

🍅 Instead of ham, you can add shrimp to the egg mixture.

🍅 Tomatoes stuffed with scrambled eggs can also be served as a cold appetizer. In this case, fry the egg mixture in a pan, let cool, and spoon into the tomatoes. Serve with a baguette.

## Mozzarella Spinach Filling

*For 8 beefsteak tomatoes: 2 tbs currants, 1 cup fresh spinach,
2 cloves garlic, 1½ tbs butter, Salt, Freshly ground pepper,
1 cup mozzarella, Oil for the casserole dish,
1 tbs grated Parmesan, 3 tbs bread crumbs*

Pour a little hot water onto the currants and soak for 10 minutes. Rinse spinach thoroughly and remove thick ribs. Wilt in boiling water, remove, rinse under cold water, and squeeze out thoroughly. Peel and chop garlic. In a pan, melt butter and sauté garlic briefly. Add spinach, season with salt and pepper, and sauté for 2 minutes, while stirring constantly. Add drained currants. Dice mozzarella and add to spinach. Transfer mixture to prepared tomatoes. Place tomatoes in an oiled casserole dish. Drizzle with oil, sprinkle with a mixture of Parmesan and bread crumbs, and bake in an oven preheated to 400°F for 15 minutes.

## Filling alla Calabrese

*For 8 tomatoes: ½ cup stale white bread, 2 cloves garlic,
6 tbs cold-pressed olive oil, 2 oz anchovy fillets, 2 oz pine nuts,
3 tbs golden raisins, 2 tbs chopped parsley, Freshly ground pepper,
Grease for the casserole dish, 1 bunch arugula*

Remove crust from bread. Peel garlic, squeeze through a press, and spread onto bread. Dice bread and fry in olive oil until lightly browned. Drain on paper towels. Soak anchovy fillets in water and mash with a fork. Combine anchovies, bread cubes, pine nuts, raisins and parsley, season with pepper, and spoon mixture into prepared tomatoes. Cover tomatoes with their caps. Preheat oven to 400°F. Grease a casserole dish, place the tomatoes inside, and bake for 20–25 minutes. Rinse arugula, spin dry, and spread on a platter. Arrange finished tomatoes on top and serve.

## Escargot Filling

*For 4 beefsteak tomatoes: 24 escargots (canned),
¼ cup herb butter, 6 tsp grated cheese (e.g., Gouda),
4 small slices cheese for melting on top (e.g., Gouda),
Butter for the casserole dish*

Drain snails, setting aside the liquid. Combine herb butter with a little snail liquid and process with grated cheese into a soft paste. Cut snails into smaller pieces and knead into the paste. Spoon into tomatoes. Cut cheese slices to the size of lids and place on top of tomatoes. Place tomatoes in a buttered casserole dish and bake in an oven preheated to 400°F until the cheese on top is slightly melted and browned (15–20 minutes).

## Middle Eastern Filling

For this filling, you will need the juice from the hollowed-out tomatoes plus, possibly, additional commercial tomato juice.

*For 4–6 beefsteak tomatoes: 1½ cups tomato juice,
3 tbs lemon juice, ½ cup stock, 1–2 bunches Italian parsley,
1 clove garlic, 1 bunch green onions, 4 tbs cold-pressed olive oil,
⅔ cup large-grain couscous, Salt, Freshly ground pepper,
Tabasco sauce, 2 organic limes, 1 tbs honey, Several lettuce leaves*

Combine tomato juice, lemon juice, and stock. Rinse parsley, pat dry, remove leaves from stems, and chop coarsely. Peel garlic, clean green onions, slice both thinly, and brown briefly in 2 tbs oil. Add couscous and sauté while stirring. Add liquid mixture, stir, and let stand for 10 minutes. Add salt and pepper, and fold in parsley and season with a few dashes of Tabasco.

Grate the peel from 1 lime and squeeze out juice. Peel the other lime, including the white membrane, and cut out segments. Combine grated peel, juice, honey, and remaining olive oil to make a dressing. Stir lime segments into the couscous, drizzle with dressing, and spoon into tomatoes. Cover tomatoes with their caps and serve on lettuce leaves.

## Warm Feta Tomatoes

For this appetizer, you will need four large soufflé dishes. If you don't have any, you can make them yourself from a double-layer of aluminum foil.

*4 large beefsteak tomatoes, 7 oz feta, ½ bunch parsley,*
*4 tsp chopped basil, Salt, Freshly ground white pepper,*
*Cold-pressed olive oil*

Brush soufflé dishes with oil. Blanch tomatoes, peel, remove cores, and slice (first cut larger tomatoes in half). Slice feta and alternately arrange tomato and feta slices in the dishes in a fan shape. Rinse parsley, pat dry, remove leaves, and chop. Sprinkle parsley and basil on top of tomatoes. Season with salt and pepper and drizzle with oil. Bake in an oven preheated to 400°F for 10 minutes, then broil briefly if necessary. Serve with small, warm party rolls.

You can also mix a little grated peel from an untreated lemon into the chopped parsley.

## Mini Quiches

Mini quiches are a pretty, fast finger food. The necessary tartlet shells can be purchased in a round or oval shape.

*Filling for 4 quiches: ¼ cup dried tomatoes, ½ cup milk,*
*2 eggs, ¼ cup crumbled goat cheese, 3 tbs chopped basil,*
*Salt, Freshly ground pepper*

Chop dried tomatoes finely. Whisk together milk and eggs. Combine goat cheese, tomatoes, eggs and basil, season with salt and pepper, and pour into tartlet shells. Bake in an oven preheated to 400°F for 15–20 minutes until golden.

# SOUPS & STEWS

## Chilled Tomato Soup

*3 beefsteak tomatoes, ¼ pkg granulated gelatin (about ¼ tbs),*
*3 cups meat stock, 4 tsp sherry, 3 tbs ketchup (recipe on page 106),*
*1 tbs lemon juice, Tabasco sauce, Salt, Sugar, 4 stalks basil,*
*8–12 ice cubes, 2 tbs crème fraîche★*

Blanch tomatoes, peel, cut into quarters, and remove cores and seeds, setting aside any juice. Dice flesh finely. Soften gelatin in a little cold water.

Combine diced tomato, tomato juice and meat stock, and bring to a boil. Squeeze out gelatin and dissolve in liquid. Add sherry, ketchup, lemon juice and Tabasco, and season to taste with salt and sugar. Refrigerate for 2 hours. In the meantime, rinse basil, pat dry, and remove leaves from stems. Set aside several leaves for garnish, cut the rest into strips, and stir into the soup before serving.

Place 2–3 ice cubes in each soup cup and ladle soup over the top. Place a dollop of crème fraîche in the center and stir it into a spiral pattern with a spoon handle. Garnish with basil leaves.

★ Crème fraîche is available in gourmet shops, or can be made by combining 1 cup whipping cream with 2 tbs buttermilk in a covered glass container at room temperature, about 70°F. Let stand for 8 to 24 hours, or until very thick.

If you want to add a garnish, this soup tastes great with shrimp. Instead of basil, you can also use chervil.

## Andalusian Gazpacho I

Sunny Spain is an ideal place for tomatoes. Throughout the summer months, tomato festivals are held on both the mainland and the islands. The festival in Buñol, for example, has achieved national fame. A fight that broke out among participants in a parade 50 years ago ended in a tomato fight between the rivals. This battle became a tradition. Every year, visitors come from all around to experience a "tomatina."

Just as famous is the gazpacho. It is in no way a new dish. A similar soup—though, of course, as yet without tomatoes—was already present in Greek and Roman literature as drinkable nourishment. When temperatures in Andalusia reach 100+°F, it often serves as a pleasant meal at lunchtime. It must be well chilled! You can easily vary the two different styles described below.

*Serves 4–6:*
*1 stale roll, 4 ripe beefsteak tomatoes,*
*½ cucumber, 1 red bell pepper, 1 onion, 3 cloves garlic,*
*5–6 tbs cold-pressed olive oil, 4 tbs sherry, Juice of 1 lime,*
*Salt, Freshly ground pepper, 1–2 cups defatted stock,*
*One stalk Italian parsley or fresh oregano*

Soften roll in water and then squeeze out. Remove cores from tomatoes. Peel cucumber. Remove stem, seeds, and interiors from bell pepper. Peel onion and garlic. Coarsely chop all these ingredients and purée in a blender. Stir in olive oil, sherry vinegar and lime juice, and season with salt and pepper. Pour in stock and refrigerate. Rinse parsley or oregano, pat dry, remove leaves from stems, and chop. Serve gazpacho sprinkled with fresh herbs.

## Andalusian Gazpacho II

*For the gazpacho: 2 slices stale white bread,*
*2¼ lb juicy ripe tomatoes (about 4½ cups),*
*2 red bell peppers, 1 onion, 2 cloves garlic,*
*1 tbs sherry vinegar, 6 tbs cold-pressed olive oil,*
*2 cups defatted stock, Salt, Lemon pepper*
*For the soup garnish: 1 red bell pepper,*
*2 tomatoes, ½ cucumber, 2 hard-boiled eggs,*
*2 slices fresh white bread, Olive oil for frying,*
*7 tbs cooked ham (about 3½ oz),*
*4 tbs pitted black olives, Ice cubes*

For the gazpacho: Soften bread briefly in water and then squeeze out. Blanch tomatoes, peel, remove cores, and hollow out over strainer, setting aside any juice. Chop flesh coarsely. Remove stems, seeds and interiors from bell peppers, and roast under the broiler with the skin side up until dark-brown. Then peel and chop coarsely. Peel onion and cut in half. Peel garlic. In a blender, purée bread, tomatoes, bell peppers, onion, and garlic. Gradually add tomato juice, vinegar, oil, and stock—the soup must be thick. Spice it up with salt and lemon pepper and refrigerate.

For the soup garnish: Remove stem, seeds, and interior from bell pepper. Remove cores from tomatoes and dice. Peel cucumber and dice. Peel and chop eggs. Dice bread and toast in a little olive oil. Cut ham into small pieces. Transfer all ingredients, including olives, to separate bowls.

Pour gazpacho into a tureen, add ice cubes and arrange bowls of diced ingredients all around. Each person can now select garnishes and ladle the soup over the top.

## Spicy Tomato Carrot Soup

*1 onion, 1¾ cups carrots (about 14 oz), 1 fresh red chile pepper,*
*3⅓ cups tomatoes, 2 tbs cold-pressed olive oil,*
*2 cups vegetable stock, 3 tbs orange juice, 2 star anise,*
*3 crushed cardamom pods, 2 tsp honey,*
*Salt, Freshly ground pepper, 1 tsp coriander, 1 tsp cumin,*
*½ cup very small cherry tomatoes, ½ bunch cilantro or mint*

Peel and dice onion. Clean carrots and coarsely chop two-thirds of them. Grate the other third, blanch briefly, and set aside. Slit open chile pepper, remove stem, seeds and interiors, and cut into pieces. Remove cores from tomatoes and cut into eighths. In a pot, heat olive oil and brown onion, coarsely chopped carrots, and chile pepper. Add tomatoes, stock, and orange juice. Place star anise and cardamom in a tea filter bag, tie shut, and add to vegetables. Season with honey, salt, pepper, coriander, and cumin. Cover and simmer for 25 minutes. Remove bundle of herbs and purée soup in a blender.

Before serving soup, either refrigerate or reheat. Add cherry tomatoes and grated carrots. Rinse cilantro or mint, pat dry, and remove leaves from stems. Season soup to taste once again, transfer to soup plates or cups, and garnish with cilantro or mint leaves. Serve with fresh flatbread.

🍅 Serve this soup ice-cold in summer and hot in winter.

🍅 Give the soup an Asian flair by adding 1 can unsweetened coconut milk (about 14 oz) and 1 crushed garlic clove. In this case, however, reduce the amount of stock. Garnish with grated coconut.

# Consommé—Clear Tomato Soup

Consommé is an elegant opening for a festive meal. You can prepare it days in advance without salt or herbs, freeze it, and heat it up when needed. It is also delicious ice-cold, refreshing and light.

*2¾ lb very ripe tomatoes (about 5½ cups), 2 cloves garlic,*
*2 small onions, 1 small chile pepper, 1 cup dry Italian red wine,*
*1 cup defatted chicken stock, Salt, 1 pinch sugar (optional),*
*Chopped herbs for garnish (e.g., basil, parsley, or chives)*

Remove cores from tomatoes and cut into quarters. Peel and chop garlic and onions. Cut chile pepper in half and remove stem, seeds, and interiors. In a pot, combine all vegetables with red wine and stock but without seasonings. Simmer for 20 minutes and then let cool slightly in the pot for 10 minutes. Line a fine-mesh strainer with cheesecloth and suspend it over a pot or bowl. Strain the soup but don't squeeze through the cloth or else the soup won't be clear! Even better is to make the soup a day ahead and let the soup drain through the cloth overnight.

Heat clear tomato soup and season to taste with salt. Serve in small cups and sprinkled with herbs. If you want to add ingredients, serve in soup plates or cups.

- Heat small ravioli (from the refrigerated section at the supermarket) separately from the soup and add just before serving.

- Egg custard cubes: Whisk together 2 eggs, ½ cup heavy cream, and a little salt. Pour into a shallow greased glass container and let set over a hot double boiler. Cut into cubes. Place 1 tbs egg cubes in each bowl, pour soup over the top, and sprinkle with herbs.

- Soak dried tomatoes in a little water, simmer for 10 minutes, cut into cubes, and sprinkle over the soup.

# Italian Tomato Soup

This soup makes a spicy, warming meal that is especially welcome on cold winter days.

*2 large onions, 1 cup fresh mushrooms, 1½ tbs butter,*
*1 clove garlic, 1 large can peeled tomatoes,*
*2 cups hearty stock, Dried herbs (e.g., oregano, thyme, marjoram),*
*Salt, Freshly ground pepper, Sugar, 2 fresh tomatoes,*
*½ cup heavy cream, Juice of 1 lemon,*
*Grated Parmesan or chopped parsley*

Peel onions and cut into paper-thin rings. Clean mushrooms and cut into halves or quarters, depending on their size. In a large pot, heat butter and brown onions and mushrooms. Peel garlic, squeeze through a press, and add. Add juice from the canned tomatoes. Chop canned tomatoes and add to soup along with stock and herbs. Season with salt, pepper and sugar, and boil thoroughly. Blanch fresh tomatoes, peel, remove cores, chop, and heat in the soup only briefly. Season to taste once again. Whip cream until not completely stiff and then add lemon juice. Place a dollop of cream on each serving of soup and sprinkle with either cheese or chopped parsley. Serve with warm rolls or freshly toasted bread.

# Provençal Tomato Soup

*2 cups chicken stock, 2¼ lb ripe tomatoes (about 4½ cups),*
*2 stalks each of lavender, rosemary, and thyme, 2 onions,*
*2 cloves garlic, 3 tbs butter, 1 tbs tomato paste,*
*½ tsp dried herbes de Provence, Salt, Freshly ground pepper,*
*Sugar, 4 tsp French herb cream cheese (e.g., Le Tartare from a gourmet*
*cheese shop or a full-fat American variety), 2 tsp heavy cream*

Heat chicken stock, add tomatoes and rinsed herb stalks, and simmer until tender. Pass through a strainer. Peel onions and garlic and chop finely. In a pot, melt butter and braise diced onion and garlic very briefly until translucent. Pour in strained soup. Add tomato paste and season with herbes de Provence, salt, pepper, and sugar.

Cook soup thoroughly. Stir together cheese and cream until smooth. Serve soup in cups with a dollop of cheese cream in the center of each.

🍅 For a heartier version, also brown 3½ tbs diced ham. In this case, be sure to reduce the amount of salt! Add 1 dash of Tabasco.

🍅 Yet another variant: Briefly heat 1 cup freshly squeezed orange juice and 6 tbs cognac. Serve with shrimp, if desired.

## Parisian Tomato Soup

This soup is obviously based on the onion soup typical of Parisian market halls.

*6 fully ripe beefsteak tomatoes, 2 onions, 1½ tbs butter,*
*1 cup white wine, Several threads saffron, 1 quart stock,*
*1 dash ground bay leaf, Salt, Freshly ground black pepper,*
*8 slices baguette, Oil for the baking sheet,*
*3½ oz grated cheese (e.g., Gouda, Gruyère, or Emmenthaler)*

Blanch tomatoes, peel, cut into quarters, and remove cores and seeds, setting aside any juice. Dice flesh. Peel and dice onions. In a pot, melt butter and sweat onions. Add wine, bring to a boil, add saffron, and reduce over high heat. Remove saffron threads. Add diced tomato, juice, and stock. Season with bay leaf, salt and pepper, and simmer for 15 minutes. Mash soup ingredients slightly to make it creamy.

Place baguette slices on an oiled baking sheet, sprinkle with a thick layer of cheese and bake in the oven at 400°F until golden. Pour soup into soup plates and place 2 browned baguette slices in each.

🍅 Instead of grated cheese, melt goat cheese onto the baguette slices.

## Swiss Velouté Soup

This soup should be smooth and zesty but not too spicy. Note that tomato soups prepared with cream or milk should always be stirred into the cream or milk. If you pour cream or milk into the boiling soup, it may curdle slightly due to the acid content of the tomatoes.

*2¼ lb very ripe, juicy tomatoes (about 4½ cups),*
*1 cup meat stock, 2 stalks tarragon, 1 cup milk,*
*2 cups heavy cream, Salt, Sugar, Hungarian sweet paprika*

Rinse tarragon. In a pot, combine tomatoes, stock and tarragon, and boil until the tomatoes disintegrate. Put through a strainer. Combine milk and cream and bring to a boil. Pour in strained tomatoes, while stirring constantly. Season to taste with salt and sugar. Rinse out soup cups with hot water, fill with soup, dust with a little paprika, and serve immediately.

# Westphalian Tomato Stew

Our grandmothers were crazy about this hearty and inexpensive stew!

*Serves 4–6:*
*2 large onions, 2 carrots, 1 large or 2 small leeks,*
*1 lb potatoes, 8 oz bratwurst, 4 small coarse-ground fresh sausages,*
*1 tbs lard, 6 cups stock, 2¼ lb ripe beefsteak tomatoes (about 4½ cups),*
*1 lb cherry tomatoes, 2 leaves lovage (or substitute celery leaves),*
*1 tbs thyme leaves, Salt, Freshly ground pepper,*
*½ bunch parsley (or 1 bunch chives)*

Peel onions and dice coarsely. Clean carrots and dice or cut into strips. Clean leek, rinse thoroughly, and cut into pieces ¾- to 1¼-inch long. Peel potatoes, rinse, and dice coarsely.

Squeeze bratwurst out of the casings and shape into small meatballs. Cut sausages into slices the same size as the meatballs. In a large pot, melt lard and slowly braise chopped vegetables and sausage. Add stock and heat.

In the meantime, pour hot water over beefsteak and cherry tomatoes and peel. Remove cores from beefsteak tomatoes and chop coarsely. Set aside cherry tomatoes. Add beefsteak tomatoes to the soup and stir well. Rinse lovage leaves, pat dry, and tear into small pieces. Add lovage and thyme to the stew, season to taste with salt and pepper, and simmer gently for 10–15 minutes.

Rinse parsley or chives and pat dry. Remove parsley leaves from stems and chop, or chop chives and stir into the soup. Then add cherry tomatoes. Do not cook them too long or at too high a heat, otherwise, they will fall apart.

If desired, serve grated cheese on the side for sprinkling on the soup.

# Basque Fish Soup

This soup, called "Ttoro" by the Basque, requires a little effort because of the step-by-step preparation. As an appetizer, it serves six, and as a main dish, it serves four. It tastes best if you prepare it a day ahead of time so the fish is well marinated.

*For the fish: 2 cups chicken stock,*
*1 tbs fish spice mixture (prepackaged 5-spice powder*
*is available in Asian markets and most supermarkets),*
*8 juniper berries, 1 bay leaf,*
*2¼ lb ocean fish fillet (e.g., cod, hake; about 4½ cups)*
*For the soup: 2–3 cloves garlic, 2 onions,*
*2¼ lb tomatoes (about 4½ cups), 1 fennel bulb,*
*4–5 stalks celery, 2 tbs cold-pressed olive oil,*
*1 cup chicken stock, 1 cup white wine, Salt,*
*2–3 tsp Italian spice mixture (e.g., thyme and chopped chile peppers)*

For the fish: Combine chicken stock, fish spice, juniper berries and bay leaf, and bring to a boil. Rinse fish, pat dry, and soak in stock that is no longer boiling until cooked. Remove and set aside. Pour liquid through a strainer and set aside.

For the soup: Peel garlic and mince. Peel onions and dice finely. Blanch tomatoes, peel, remove cores, chop coarsely, and purée in a blender. Clean fennel and celery and cut into bite-sized pieces.

In a large pot, heat olive oil and briefly braise garlic, onions, fennel, and celery. Add stock and wine and stir in tomato purée. Season with salt and spice mixture and cook thoroughly for 10 minutes.

Divide fish into bite-sized pieces and add to soup along with the set aside fish liquid. Heat but do not boil. Stir very gently. Serve with rye rolls and flatbread.

🍅 You can also add shrimp and/or mussels, as desired.

# Caldeirada

Caldeirada is a specialty of Portugal. The name refers to a fish ragout or goulash. In Chile, this same dish is called Caldillo. There it is mainly prepared with conger eel (congrio) and it is not baked in the oven as it is in Portugal, but cooked on the stove. Each Portuguese province has its own recipe. This dish comes from Albufeira on the Algarve. The most important ingredient in this stew is firm ocean fish. You can use a single type or combine several different ones. At the markets on the Algarve, fish is available already cut up and cleaned so it's easier to prepare.

*Serves 6:*
*3⅓ lb ocean fish (e.g., sole, turbot, flounder, conger eel, etc.),*
*1 lb potatoes, 1 cup onions, 1 lb plum tomatoes, 2 green bell peppers,*
*2 cloves garlic, 4 tbs olive oil, 1 cup dry white wine,*
*1 small bay leaf, 1 tsp paprika, Salt, Freshly ground pepper,*
*Oil for the casserole dish, 3 slices smoked Serrano ham, Parsley for sprinkling*

Rinse fish, clean, and fillet. Don't through away fish scraps. If a helpful fish dealer does the work for you, ask if you can take the scraps with you. You will boil them in the soup.

Peel potatoes, rinse, and slice. Peel onions and cut into rings. Blanch tomatoes, peel, remove cores, and slice crosswise. Cut bell peppers in half, remove stem, seeds and interiors, and cut into strips. Peel and chop garlic.

In a large pot, heat oil and briefly roast garlic. Add 1 cup water, wine, fish scraps, bay leaf, and paprika. Bring to a boil and simmer for about 20 minutes. Then pour liquid through a fine-mesh strainer and set aside. Season liberally with salt and pepper.

Preheat oven to 400°F. Brush oil onto the bottom of a baking dish with a lid. Arrange half the potatoes in layers and follow with a layer of onions, a layer of fish, a layer of tomatoes, and paprika. Repeat the process. Pour in enough fish stock so it just reaches the top layer but doesn't cover it. Top with Serrano ham. Seal the pot well and bake in the oven for 30–40 minutes. Serve sprinkled with a lot of parsley.

## Chili con Carne

Chili con carne is a dish to warm your soul, which means it's great in winter.

*2 onions, 1 clove garlic, 1 fresh red chile pepper, 2 tbs olive oil,*
*1 lb ground beef, 2 tsp chili powder, 1 tsp cumin,*
*Salt, Freshly ground black pepper, 1 cup dried tomatoes in oil,*
*2 cans tomatoes (about 15 oz each), ½ cinnamon stick,*
*2 cups stock, 2 cans red beans (about 15 oz each), 4 tbs sour cream*

Peel and onions and garlic and dice finely. Slit open chile pepper, remove stem, seeds and interiors, and chop very finely. In a pot, heat oil and lightly brown onions, garlic, and chile pepper. Add ground beef, season with chili powder, cumin, salt and pepper, and brown thoroughly. Purée dried tomatoes with just enough oil to produce a smooth paste. Add this paste to the meat along with the canned tomatoes (including liquid), cinnamon stick, and stock. Bring to a boil and simmer for about 1 hour. Then add drained beans and heat briefly. Transfer chili to bowls and top with a dollop of sour cream. Serve with a fresh baguette or hearty flatbread.

# Aztec-Style Tomato Soup

*1 onion, 2 cloves garlic, 2 ears sweet corn,*
*4 large beefsteak tomatoes (or 14 oz canned tomatoes),*
*1 fresh chile pepper, 2 tbs corn oil, 1 quart chicken stock,*
*2 oz taco shells, 1 rip avocado, 2 limes, ⅔ cup feta,*
*7 oz sour cream, 2 tbs light whipping cream,*
*Salt, Freshly ground pepper, 1 pinch sugar*

Peel onion and garlic. Finely dice onion and squeeze garlic through a press. Strip corn from ears using a fork. Blanch tomatoes, remove cores, and dice (drain canned tomatoes). Slit open chile pepper, remove stem, seeds and interiors, and chop very finely.

In a large pot, heat oil and sweat onion, garlic, and corn kernels until translucent. Add diced tomatoes, chile pepper and stock, and simmer thoroughly for 5 minutes.

Break taco shells into small pieces. Peel avocado, remove pit, and cut flesh into thin segments or cubes. Then drizzle with the juice of 1 lime to prevent discoloration. Cut the remaining lime into quarters. Dice feta. Place lime, feta, taco shells, and avocado in separate bowls. In another bowl, stir together sour and whipping cream. Season soup with salt, pepper and sugar, and serve hot. Each person can garnish their soup as desired.

🍅 Texas Stew is prepared similarly to Aztec soup. Just add 1 cup white wine, 1 tsp coarsely ground cumin, and 1 dash cayenne pepper. Along with the other garnishes, include one bowl of grated Parmesan and another of fresh, shredded cilantro leaves.

# SALADS & SIDES

## Tomato Mozzarella Salad

This Italian tomato salad has become a classic and makes an ideal appetizer or buffet dish.

*For the salad: 3⅓ cups meaty tomatoes, 2–3 mozzarella balls,*
*3½ tbs pitted black olives (optional), Several stalks basil*
*For the dressing: ½ clove garlic, 1 tsp lemon juice or balsamic vinegar,*
*2 tbs cold-pressed olive oil, Salt, Freshly ground black pepper, 1 pinch sugar*

Remove cores from tomatoes and slice. Slice mozzarella and, if desired, olives. Rinse basil, pat dry, and remove leaves from stems.

On a platter, arrange tomato and mozzarella slices in an overlapping pattern. Sprinkle with basil leaves and olives, if desired.

For the dressing: Peel garlic and squeeze through a press. Combine lemon juice or balsamic vinegar with 1–2 tbs water and olive oil and season with salt, pepper, and sugar. Drizzle over the salad.

## Tomato Salad with Marinated Feta

Feta is traditionally made from sheep's or goat's milk and comes from Greece and the Balkans. Because of its growing popularity, it is now produced here as well, but often from cow's milk. Be sure to purchase real feta. It's available in a block of pure soft cheese or crumbled and sometimes marinated in an herb–oil–garlic brine.

*1 lb small plum tomatoes, 1 cup feta cubes in oil,*
*3 stalks basil, 3 tbs lemon juice, ½ tsp sugar*

Remove cores from tomatoes and slice crosswise. Remove feta from spiced oil and cut into smaller cubes, if necessary. Rinse basil, pat dry, remove leaves from stems, and chop coarsely.

In a wide bowl, arrange alternating layers of tomatoes and feta, sprinkling each layer with basil. Whisk together lemon juice, 2 tbs water, and 4 tbs spiced feta oil. Stir in remaining basil and sugar and drizzle over the salad. Serve salad as an appetizer with Italian breadsticks or as a side with a main dish of meat or fish.

## Greek Peasant Salad

*½ cucumber, 4 firm tomatoes, 2 small red onions, 1 green bell pepper,*
*Several stalks fresh oregano, Italian parsley, or dill,*
*3½ oz black olives, 8 tbs cold-pressed olive oil, 4 tbs lemon juice,*
*Salt, Freshly ground black pepper, 3½ oz feta cheese*

Peel cucumber and cut into thick slices. Remove cores from tomatoes and slice or cut into eighths. Peel onions and cut into thin rings. Cut bell pepper in half, remove stem, seeds and interiors, and cut into strips. Combine all these ingredients in a wide bowl. Rinse herbs, pat dry, and remove leaves from stems. Scatter olives over the salad. Combine olive oil, lemon juice, salt and pepper, and drizzle over the salad. Finally, sprinkle on herbs and diced feta.

## Panzanella—Tuscan Bread Salad

*For the salad: 1 clove garlic, 4 thick slices stale white bread,*
*3–4 tbs olive oil, 1¾ cups tomatoes (about 14 oz),*
*½ bunch green onions, ½ small cucumber, 1 small yellow bell pepper*
*For the dressing: 2 tbs wine vinegar (red or white),*
*Salt, Freshly ground pepper, 4 tbs cold-pressed olive oil,*
*1 tbs chopped parsley, 2 tbs chopped basil,*
*1 oz chopped hazelnuts or pine nuts*

For the salad: Peel garlic, cut in half crosswise, and rub onto bread slices. Dice bread and fry in olive oil until crispy and brown. Drain on paper towels. Blanch tomatoes, peel, remove cores and seeds, and dice. Clean green onions and cut diagonally into rings. Peel cucumber, cut in half lengthwise, and scrape out seeds. Dice the 2 halves. Cut bell pepper in half, remove stem, seeds and interiors, and dice.

For the dressing: Whisk together vinegar, salt, pepper, and olive oil. Stir in parsley and basil. Combine all the ingredients in a bowl, toss with dressing, and refrigerate for 15 minutes. In an ungreased pan, toast hazelnuts or pine nuts and sprinkle onto salad just before serving.

 Instead of cucumber and bell pepper, add 2 tbs very small or chopped capers and 1 bunch arugula.

# Tomato Arugula Salad

*For the salad: 3½ oz arugula, 1 cup small vine tomatoes,*
*2 oz pine nuts, 2 slices white bread, 1½ tbs butter, 4 tbs shaved Parmesan*
*For the dressing: 2 tbs balsamic vinegar, Salt, Freshly ground pepper,*
*1 pinch sugar, 3 tbs cold-pressed olive oil,*
*1 tbs each of chopped herbs (e.g., parsley, basil, lemon thyme),*
*2 green onions, 2–3½ tbs shaved Parmesan*

For the salad: Rinse arugula, pat dry, and remove hard stems. Remove cores from tomatoes and cut into quarters. In an ungreased pan, toast pine nuts without browning. Dice bread and sauté in butter until crispy.

For the dressing: Combine balsamic vinegar, 2 tbs water, salt, pepper, sugar, and olive oil. Clean and finely chop green onions and add to dressing along with herbs. Transfer arugula and tomatoes to a wide bowl and sprinkle with pine nuts and croutons. Pour on dressing and toss once gently. Serve sprinkled with shaved Parmesan.

## Middle Eastern Tomato Cucumber Salad

Like many Middle Eastern dishes, this one uses couscous. Couscous is a North African grain specialty made from wheat or millet that must (like semolina) be soaked in water. To guarantee success, follow the instructions on the package. In the southeastern Mediterranean region, couscous is used both as a warm side and as a base for cold salads.

*For the salad: 1/3 cup couscous (instant), 1 3/4 cups tomatoes (about 14 oz), 1 small cucumber, 3 tbs cold-pressed olive oil, 1/2 tsp cumin*
*For the dressing: 1 small container plain yogurt, Salt, Freshly ground pepper, 1 tbs chopped dill, 1 tbs chopped mint*

For the salad: Pour boiling water over couscous as per the package instructions and let stand and cool. Remove cores from tomatoes and dice. Peel cucumber, cut in half lengthwise, scrape out seeds with a spoon, and dice the 2 halves. In a bowl, toss diced tomatoes and cucumber with olive oil. Using 2 forks, fluff couscous and mix with the salad. Season liberally with cumin.

For the dressing: Beat yogurt until fluffy and whisk together with salt, pepper, and herbs. If the dressing isn't liquidy enough, stir in a little milk. Pour dressing over the salad and serve well chilled.

# Tabouleh

Tabouleh is one of the many appetizers served in Lebanon as part of a "mazza." It gets its wonderfully nutty flavor from bulghur, which is wheat cooked until it bursts. It is then dried in the sun and crushed or ground more or less finely. Bulghur is available in health food stores and Middle Eastern markets.

There are various ways to prepare tabouleh. Many salads contain diced bell pepper and cucumber, whereas others have none or only some of these ingredients. In any case, the salad is always green with parsley. This recipe gives you a lot of room to vary the ingredients.

*3½ oz bulghur (medium to coarse), 1⅓ cups tomatoes (about 10½ oz),*
*1 medium red onion (or 3 green onions), 2 bunches Italian parsley,*
*4 stalks mint, Juice of 2 lemons, 4 tbs cold-pressed olive oil,*
*Salt, Freshly ground black pepper*

Pour bulghur into a bowl and cover with cold water. Let stand for at least 1 hour. Pour into a strainer and rinse under running water, then thoroughly squeeze out liquid.

Blanch tomatoes, peel, remove cores and seeds, and dice. Peel onion and dice finely (clean green onions and chop, including green part). Rinse herbs, pat dry, remove leaves from stems, and chop. Whisk together lemon juice, olive oil, salt, and pepper. Combine all the ingredients in a bowl.

 If you can't find bulghur, use durum wheat semolina or cooked rice.

## Tomato Banana Salad

This is my family's favorite salad! It tastes fantastic with fried chicken, steak, or fish fillets.

*For the salad: 1 lb plum tomatoes, 3–4 bananas*
*For the dressing: 2 tbs lemon juice, 2 tbs sunflower oil,*
*1 pinch salt, Freshly ground pepper*
*Plus: 2 tbs chopped parsley or chives*

For the salad: Remove cores from tomatoes and slice. Peel bananas and slice.

For the dressing: Combine lemon juice, 2 tbs water and sunflower oil, and season with salt and pepper.

Layer tomato and banana slices in a bowl, pouring dressing onto each layer. Carefully toss salad before serving. Sprinkle with parsley or chives.

🍅 Add shrimp to turn this salad into a quick and elegant appetizer.

# Dutch Salad

This salad can be served either as a refreshing appetizer or as a filling side with light meat or fish dishes.

*For the salad: 1 lb plum tomatoes, 4 hard-boiled eggs,*
*1 cup cooked ham, 3½ oz young Gouda or Edam*
*For the dressing: 1 small onion, Juice of 1 lemon, ½ cup heavy cream,*
*1 tbs capers, 1 tbs dill tips, Salt, Freshly ground pepper,*
*1 pinch sugar, 1 dash Tabasco sauce*

Remove cores from tomatoes and slice. Peel eggs and dice coarsely. Dice ham. Remove rind from cheese and dice. Layer ingredients in a bowl.

For the dressing: Peel and chop onion. Combine lemon juice and cream. Add onion, capers and dill tips, and season to taste with salt, pepper, sugar, and Tabasco until spicy and slightly hot. Drizzle dressing over the salad and marinate for 2 hours before serving.

# Provençal Tomato Salad

*For the salad: 1 lb tomatoes, 1⅓ cups zucchini (about 10½ oz), 1 onion*
*For the dressing: 1 egg yolk, 1 tsp lemon juice, Salt, Freshly ground pepper,*
*½ cup cold-pressed olive oil, 1 tbs dry white wine,*
*1 tbs finely chopped black olives, 1 tsp dried herbes de Provence*

For the salad: Remove cores from tomatoes and slice. Clean zucchini and slice thinly. Peel onion and slice or cut into rings. Combine vegetables in a bowl.

Allow all the dressing ingredients to reach room temperature. Beat egg yolk and lemon juice until smooth and season with salt and pepper. Gradually add olive oil while stirring constantly to produce a smooth mayonnaise. Stir in wine, olives, and herbs. Pour dressing over the salad and toss gently.

## Tomato Rice

*1 large onion, 3 tbs olive oil, 1 cup long-grain rice, 2 cups boiling water,*
*1 cup tomatoes, 1 tsp salt, 1 tsp Hungarian sweet paprika*

Peel onion and cut into rings. In a large pot, heat oil and braise onion over low heat, while stirring constantly for about 5 minutes until translucent. Add rice and sauté briefly. Then pour in boiling water and let stand for 5 minutes.

In the meantime, blanch tomatoes, peel, remove cores and seeds, and dice. Stir into the rice, season with salt and paprika, stir again, and cover. Cook rice over low heat for about 15 minutes until it has soaked up all the liquid.

Instead of rice, you can also prepare this dish with bulghur. Bulghur is handled in the same way as rice but with a total preparation time of only 10 minutes.

## Baked Polenta alla Calabrese

*2 tsp salt, 1⅓ cups coarse polenta, 1 onion, 2¼ lb beefsteak tomatoes,*
*3½ tbs butter, ½ cup stock, ½ tsp ground bay leaf,*
*Salt, Freshly ground pepper, Grease for the baking dish,*
*3½ oz freshly grated Parmesan or pecorino cheese*

In a saucepan, bring 1½ quarts water to a boil, add salt, and gradually pour in polenta while stirring. Let expand for 15 minutes while stirring constantly. Spread finished polenta onto a baking sheet in a layer the thickness of a finger and let cool.

In the meantime, peel and dice onion. Blanch tomatoes, peel, remove cores, and chop. In a pan, melt 1½ tbs butter, sweat onion until translucent, and then add tomatoes. Pour in stock, season with bay leaf, salt and pepper, and cook for 15 minutes.

Grease a baking dish. Fill with alternating layers of polenta, tomato sauce, and Parmesan. Finish with a layer of tomato sauce, cheese, and remaining butter cut into bits. Cook in an oven preheated to 400°F for about 30 minutes. Serve with cutlets, salad, and a dry white wine.

# Baked Tomatoes

*8 tomatoes uniform size, 2 onions, 1 tart apple (e.g., Jonathan),*
*3 tbs butter, 1 tsp sugar, 1 tbs fresh chopped tarragon or 1 tsp dried tarragon,*
*½ cup white wine, Salt, Freshly ground pepper, ½ bunch parsley*

Blanch tomatoes, peel, and remove cores by cutting out a wedge with the tip of a knife. Peel and chop onions. Peel apple, remove core, and grate. In a pan, heat half the butter, sauté onions, and season with sugar and tarragon.
Add apple and toss briefly in the butter. Add white wine and simmer to loosen pan residues. Pour liquid into a baking dish. Place tomatoes side by side in the dish and top each tomato with a flake of butter. Season with salt and pepper. Bake in an oven preheated to 400°F until the tomatoes are tender and the onions in the liquid are nicely browned. In the meantime, rinse parsley, pat dry, remove leaves from stems, and chop. Just before serving, sprinkle parsley over the tomatoes.

## Pan-Fried Tomatoes and Onions

For this dish, the tomatoes and onions should be as large as possible.

*1²⁄₃ cups onions, 2 tsp salt, 1 tbs wine vinegar, 1 lb tomatoes,*
*Salt, Freshly ground pepper, Paprika, ¹⁄₃ cup butter*

Peel onions and simmer in 2 cups salted water and vinegar for 10 minutes. Remove and drain. Blanch tomatoes, peel, cut an X through the skin on the top of each, and remove core. Sprinkle with salt, pepper, and paprika. In a pan, melt butter and sauté onions until lightly browned. Shake the pan occasionally so the onions brown on all sides. Add tomatoes, cover, and braise over low heat for about 15 minutes until done.

🍅 Instead of onions, use 2 large leeks cut into pieces.

## Warm Provençal Tomatoes

*10 medium meaty tomatoes, 3 tbs butter,*
*Salt, Freshly ground pepper, 2 tbs bread crumbs,*
*2 tbs grated cheese (Gruyère or Emmenthaler),*
*¹⁄₂ tbs dried herbes de Provence*

Cut tomatoes in half crosswise and remove cores. Butter a casserole dish. Place tomato halves in the casserole dish with the cut sides up and season with salt and pepper. Combine bread crumbs, cheese and herbs, and sprinkle over tomatoes. Top with remaining butter cut into bits. Brown in an oven preheated to 425°F for 15 minutes.

Provençal tomatoes make a great light vegetarian entrée or a delicious side dish with lamb chops or pork tenderloin.

# Ratatouille

Ratatouille is actually a hearty gypsy dish from Provence. Originally called Boumiano, it quickly spread all around the Mediterranean and is now known worldwide in many different versions. On the Riviera, it is served hot or cold with a baguette as a complete lunch. However, this vegetable dish also makes an excellent side dish with roasts, grilled meat, or fish dishes.

*Serves 6:*
*2 onions, 2 cloves garlic, 2 red and 2 green bell peppers,*
*2 small eggplant, 3 small zucchini, 1 lb small firm tomatoes,*
*5 tbs olive oil, Salt, Freshly ground pepper,*
*1 tsp dried herbes de Provence,*
*1 tbs white wine vinegar, 1 stalk basil*

Peel onions and garlic and chop finely. Cut bell peppers in half and remove stems, seeds, and interiors. Dice eggplant and zucchini and cut all the vegetables into bite-sized pieces. Blanch tomatoes, peel, remove cores, and cut into quarters.

In a large roasting pan, heat olive oil and begin by braising onion and garlic until translucent. Then add peppers, zucchini and eggplant, and brown lightly. Add tomatoes, stir, and season with salt, pepper, herbes de Provence, and vinegar. Cover, reduce heat, and braise for 10 minutes. You may have to add water if the tomatoes don't yield enough juice. In the meantime, rinse basil, pat dry, remove leaves from stems, and cut into strips. Add to ratatouille, stir gently, and season to taste. Don't let the vegetables become too soft.

When the Spanish prepare braised tomatoes with vegetables, they don't necessarily use zucchini and eggplant, but often use celery instead. They refine the flavor with grated lemon peel and several dashes of lemon juice and eat it with omelets. I know a version from Andalusia made with mushrooms, bell peppers, carrots, tomatoes, and onions. Now you know how versatile ratatouille can be. Just use your favorite vegetables.

## Tomatoes and Fennel

*2 large onions, 4 large fennel bulbs, 4 cloves garlic,*
*1 tbs cold-pressed olive oil, 3½ tbs diced streaky bacon,*
*½ cup white wine, 6 tomatoes,*
*½ tsp ground bay leaf, Salt, Freshly ground pepper*

Peel onions and cut into quarters. Clean fennel bulbs and cut into quarters, removing the core. Set aside fennel greens. Peel garlic and slice very thinly. In a pan, heat olive oil and sauté onions and bacon until golden. Add fennel and garlic and braise briefly. Pour in wine. Simmer and reduce liquid by half. In the meantime, blanch tomatoes, peel, remove cores, and cut into quarters. Add to vegetables and season with bay leaf, salt, and pepper. Simmer uncovered for 15 minutes, then cover, turn off the burner, and let stand for another 10 minutes. Serve vegetables sprinkled with chopped fennel leaves. This tastes great with lamb chops and penne rigate.

## Green Tomatoes and Bacon

Green tomatoes are both a variety of tomato and an unripe red tomato. The unripe tomatoes are not edible raw but can be eaten cooked. This American dish makes a delicious side.

*8 slices bacon, 4 medium green tomatoes, 1 egg,*
*Flour, Salt, Freshly ground pepper, 1 onion*

In a pan, fry bacon on both sides until crispy and brown. Remove and let cool on paper towels. Set aside pan.

Remove cores from tomatoes and cut into slices ¼-inch thick. In a shallow bowl, beat egg until foamy. Spread a little flour in another shallow bowl. Dredge tomato slices in the egg and then in flour. Fry tomatoes in bacon grease on both sides until brown. Season with salt and pepper, remove from pan, and keep warm on a platter. Peel onion, cut into rings, and fry. Distribute onion rings over the tomatoes. Crumble bacon and sprinkle on top.

# PIZZAS & HEARTY TORTES

## Italian Pizza

Pizza as we know it is actually a deluxe version of what was originally a simple Italian flatbread. Over time, this bread was refined with all sorts of toppings. First the dough was rolled out, drizzled with olive oil, and topped with slices of tomato and mozzarella. Then the flatbread was spread with tomato sauce and topped with salami or ham slices. Seafood also became a favorite topping. But no matter what, there was always tomatoes, mozzarella, and grated Parmesan or pecorino. Today, classic ingredients also include olives, anchovies, and the seasonings, either dried or fresh, oregano, thyme, and marjoram.

*1 cup flour, 1½ tbs yeast, 1 pinch salt,*
*1 pinch sugar, ½ cup lukewarm water, 4 tbs oil*

Sift flour into a bowl and make a well in the center. Crumble yeast into a cup, sprinkle with salt and sugar, stir with lukewarm water until smooth, and pour into the well. Add 1 tbs oil and carefully knead into a smooth dough. Cover and set aside in a warm place for 30 minutes. Then knead thoroughly, roll out on a floured surface into a thin sheet, and transfer to an oiled baking sheet. Brush with olive oil and top as desired. Bake in an oven preheated to 475°F for about 15 minutes.

As pizza toppings you can use, for example: Classic Tomato Sauce (recipe on page 97), Sauce Napoletana (recipe on page 98), Bolognese Sauce (recipe on page 99), tuna, shrimp, cooked ham, salami, onions, bell peppers, mushrooms, artichoke hearts, spinach, asparagus, olives, and capers. Classic combinations include:

| | |
|---|---|
| Pizza Margherita: | (named after an Italian queen): Tomatoes, mozzarella, fresh basil |
| Pizza Napoletana: | Tomatoes, mozzarella, anchovy fillets, oregano, olive oil |
| Pizza Milano: | Tomato sauce, ham, olives, pecorino, oregano |
| Pizza Quattro Stagioni: | Tomatoes, mozzarella, mushrooms, cooked ham, artichoke hearts, black olives |
| Pizza Siciliana: | Tomatoes, mozzarella, bell peppers, salami, mushrooms |

## American Pizza

For the dough, use twice as much yeast as for Italian Pizza (recipe on page 55) and let it rise twice on the baking sheet. Top it after it rises the first time, then let it rise again, and bake in an oven preheated to 350°F for 15–20 minutes. There is no end to the variety of toppings possible (for example, ham and pineapple or salami and pepperoni).

## Calzone with Tomatoes and Onions

*For the dough: 1¾ cups wheat flour, 1 tsp salt, 2 tbs yeast,*
*1 cup lukewarm water, 3 tbs olive oil*
*For the filling: 1⅓ cups onions, 3½ oz pitted black olives,*
*6 anchovy fillets, 1 tbs capers, 1⅓ cups small tomatoes (about 10½ oz),*
*1 bunch parsley, 5 tbs olive oil, Oregano, Salt, Freshly ground pepper,*
*⅔ cup grated young pecorino cheese*
*Plus: Flour for the work surface, Oil for the baking sheet, 1 egg for brushing*

For the dough: In a bowl, combine flour and salt. Dissolve yeast in water and add yeast and oil to flour. Knead into a pliable dough, shape into a ball, cover, and set aside in a warm place for 30 minutes.

For the filling: Peel onions and cut into rings. Finely chop olives, anchovy fillets, and capers. Blanch tomatoes, peel, remove cores and seeds, and dice. Rinse parsley, pat dry, and chop leaves. In a pan, heat oil. Add onions, cover, and braise until tender. Add olives, anchovies, capers, tomatoes, and parsley. Season with oregano, salt, and pepper. Let pan contents cool and stir in cheese.

Separate egg. Roll out dough on a floured surface to a thickness of about ⅜ inch. Spread filling onto one half, leaving a border around it the width of a finger around the edges, and brush border with egg white. Fold over the other half and press the edges together. Brush the border with egg white once again, fold inward, and press together. Place calzone upside-down on a greased baking sheet. Brush the surface with egg yolk. Cover and let rise for another 20 minutes. Bake in an oven preheated to 400°F for 25–30 minutes.

## Mexican Quesadillas

Precooked tortillas are available in the supermarket. With the following recipe, however, you can make your own.

*For the dough: ½ cup cornmeal, 1 tsp salt, Several drops oil*
*For the filling: 3½ oz ricotta cheese, 3 tbs sour cream,*
*1 small shallot, 3½ oz diced ham, 1 small fresh chile pepper,*
*¼ cup dried tomatoes, 1 tbs chopped cilantro, Salt, Freshly ground pepper*
*Plus: Oil for frying*

In a bowl, combine cornmeal and salt. Gradually add 1 cup water while stirring constantly. Add several drops of oil and knead into a pliable dough until it is no longer sticky. If necessary, add a little water. Roll out dough between 2 sheets of parchment paper or plastic wrap to a thickness of ⅛ inch. Cut out circles with a 5- to 6-inch diameter. In a pan, heat a generous amount of oil and fry tortillas on both sides for 2 minutes until golden. Place between layers of aluminum foil and keep warm in an oven preheated to 200°F.

For the filling: Combine ricotta and sour cream. Peel and dice shallot and add to mixture along with ham. Slit open chile pepper, remove stem, seeds and interiors, and chop very finely. Soak tomatoes in water for 10 minutes and then dice. Add chile pepper, tomatoes, and cilantro to the ricotta mixture. Season with salt and pepper.

Spread filling onto tortillas. Brush edges with water and fold tortillas in half. Press edges together with a fork. In a pan, heat oil and fry quesadillas on both sides until nice and brown. You can serve them with cold sauces (such as Mojo Rojo and Salsa Verde, recipes on pages 95–96).

🍅 Make small quesadillas and serve as canapés.

🍅 Add red beans or corn to the filling.

## Italian Tomato Torte

*For the dough: 7 tbs flour, 7 tbs rye flour, 2 tbs ice water,*
*1 egg yolk, ½ tsp salt, ⅔ cup butter*
*For the filling: 1 stale roll, 1 onion, 2¼ lb firm cherry tomatoes,*
*½ lb ground meat (half beef, half pork), 1 egg, Salt, Freshly ground pepper,*
*Hungarian sweet paprika, 3½ tbs tangy cheese (e.g., pecorino),*
*1 tbs cold-pressed olive oil, 2 tbs olive oil, 2 tbs bread crumbs*
*For the egg cream: ½ cup heavy cream,*
*½ cup milk, 4 eggs, Salt, Freshly ground pepper,*
*Paprika, 4 tbs chopped herbs as desired (e.g., basil, ore-*
*gano. parsley, chives)*
*Plus: Grease for the pan, Bread crumbs for*
*the pan and shell, Flour for the work surface,*
*Oil or melted butter for brushing*

With cold hands, quickly knead dough ingredients into a smooth dough and refrigerate for 30 minutes. Grease a springform pan with a 10-inch diameter and dust
with bread crumbs. Roll out dough on a floured surface and transfer to springform
pan, forming a high border around the edges. Bake blind in an oven preheated to
400°F for 10 minutes.

For the filling: Soak roll in a little water. Peel and chop onion. Cut a cap off the
tops of tomatoes and carefully hollow out the tomatoes themselves. Knead together
ground meat, squeezed out roll, egg, onion, salt, pepper, and paprika. Dice cheese.
Wet your hands and shape meat mixture into balls that fit inside the tomatoes.
Enclose a cube of cheese inside each meatball and place inside a tomato.

For the egg cream: Whisk together milk and eggs and season with salt, pepper, and
paprika. Stir in half the chopped herbs.

Sprinkle prebaked shell with bread crumbs. Arrange tomatoes on the shell pressed
tightly together. If you have any leftover meat, crumble it around the tomatoes.
Distribute egg cream over the top. Sprinkle with remaining herbs. Bake torte in an
oven preheated to 400°F for about 40 minutes. While the torte is still hot, brush
on a little oil or melted butter. Serve with a fresh green salad.

# Savory Tomato Cake

*For the dough: 1 cup flour, 2 tsp yeast, 5 tbs clarified butter, Salt*
*For the topping: 1 lb tomatoes, 1 lb zucchini, Salt,*
*3½ oz grated tangy cheese (e.g., Emmenthaler)*
*For the egg cream: 2 eggs, 1 container crème fraîche★ (about 4⅓ oz),*
*1 tbs chopped thyme, 1 tbs chopped marjoram or rosemary*
*Plus: Flour for the work surface, Grease for the baking sheet*

For the dough: Place flour in a bowl, make a well in the center, and crumble in the yeast. Heat clarified butter until lukewarm and liquefied. Pour into well along with salt. Knead all ingredients into a smooth dough. Cover and let rise in a warm place for 30 minutes.

For the topping: Clean tomatoes and zucchini, remove cores from tomatoes, and cut both vegetables into slices ¼-inch thick.

For the egg cream: Combine eggs and crème fraîche and stir in chopped herbs.

Roll out dough on a floured surface and transfer to a greased baking sheet, forming a low border around the edges. Let rise for another 10 minutes. Arrange alternating slices of tomato and zucchini on top in an overlapping pattern. Season with salt and sprinkle with cheese. Pour on egg cream and bake in an oven preheated to 425°F for 40 minutes.

★ Crème fraîche is available in gourmet shops, or can be made by combining 1 cup whipping cream with 2 tbs buttermilk in a covered glass container at room temperature, about 70°F. Let stand for 8 to 24 hours, or until very thick.

Toast 2½ oz pine nuts in an ungreased pan and sprinkle over cake before serving.

## Tomato Tart

*For the dough: 1 recipe dough from Tomato Quiche (recipe below)*
*For the topping: 2¼ lb cherry tomatoes, 1 onion, 7 oz sour cream,*
*1 tbs dried herbes de Provence, 2 tbs grated hard cheese (e.g., Gruyère,*
*Parmesan, etc.), Salt, Freshly ground pepper*
*Plus: Flour for the work surface, Grease for the pan, Butter*

Prepare dough according to the recipe. Roll out on a floured surface and transfer to a greased tart pan, forming a high border around the edges.

For the topping: Blanch tomatoes, peel, cut in half, and remove cores and seeds. Peel and dice onion. Combine sour cream, diced onion, herbs, and half the cheese.

Spread cream mixture onto the dough. Season tomato halves with salt and pepper and arrange in the pan with the cut sides up and pressed close together. Distribute remaining cheese and butter cut into bits on top. Bake in an oven preheated to 400°F for about 40 minutes. Serve tart warm with a fresh salad.

## Tomato Quiche

*For the dough: ⅔ cup low-fat small curd cottage cheese, 6 tbs oil,*
*7 tbs milk, 1 pinch salt, 1⅓ cups flour, 1 pinch baking powder*
*For the filling: 1⅓ cups onions (about 10½ oz), 1½ tbs butter,*
*7 oz grated Emmenthaler, 7 oz grated Gruyère, 1–2 tbs flour,*
*4 eggs, 7 oz sour cream, A little freshly ground pepper, 1 pinch grated nutmeg,*
*7 oz each of red, yellow, and green tomatoes (may substitute 21 oz red tomatoes), Ore-*
*gano, 1 bunch basil*
*Plus: Grease for the pan or baking sheet, Flour for the work surface*

For the dough: In a strainer, squeeze liquid out of cottage cheese. Combine cottage cheese, oil, milk, and salt. Work in half the flour. Combine remaining flour with baking powder and knead into cottage cheese mixture. Set aside for 30 minutes.

For the filling: Peel onions and cut into rings. In a pan, heat butter, briefly braise onion rings, and then let cool. Combine cheese and flour. Whisk together eggs and sour cream and season with pepper and nutmeg. Fold in cheese-flour mixture. Cut tomatoes in half crosswise and remove cores. Grease a quiche pan or baking sheet. On a floured surface, roll out dough into a thin sheet and transfer to the pan, forming a high border around the edges. Top with onions and cheese cream. Press tomato halves into the cheese cream with the cut sides up and pressed tightly together. Strip oregano from stems and sprinkle over top. Rinse basil, pat dry, remove leaves, and distribute over tomatoes. Bake quiche in an oven preheated to 400°F for 40–50 minutes. Delicious warm or cold. Serve with a light white wine.

## Spanish Quiche

*For the dough: 1⅔ cups flour, 1 pinch salt,*
*½ cup butter, cut into bits, ½ cup ice-water*
*For the filling: 1¾ cups tomatoes (about 14 oz), 1¾ cups onions (about 14 oz),*
*4 cloves garlic, 2 tbs oil, 1 bay leaf (or 1 dash ground bay leaf), 1 pinch dried thyme,*
*1 pinch dried rosemary, Salt, Freshly ground pepper, 3 eggs, 1 cup heavy cream*
*Plus: Grease for the pan, Flour for the work surface,*
*1 small jar pitted Spanish olives (¼–⅓ cup drained weight)*

On the day before baking, quickly knead dough ingredients with cold hands and shape into a ball. Wrap in plastic wrap and refrigerate overnight. The next day, remove from refrigerator 1 hour before processing.

Grease a quiche or springform pan with an 11-inch diameter. On a floured surface, roll out dough to the necessary size and transfer to pan, forming a high border around the edges.

For the filling: Blanch tomatoes, peel, remove stems, and chop finely. Peel onions and cut into fine rings. Peel and chop garlic. In a pan, heat oil and sweat onions and garlic. Add tomatoes, bring to a boil, and season with bay leaf, herbs, salt, and pepper. Simmer for 15 minutes. Remove bay leaf and let tomato mixture cool. Whisk together eggs and cream and stir in. Pour filling into the shell. Cut olives in half and scatter over the top. Bake in an oven preheated to 400°F for 30–40 minutes. Quiche is delicious warm as a small main meal or cold as an appetizer.

# VEGETABLE DISHES
# & CASSEROLES

## Greek-Style Stuffed Tomatoes

*1⅓ cups rice (about 10.5 oz), 2 cups stock, 12 firm beefsteak tomatoes,*
*2–3 large onions, ½ cup olive oil, 4–5 cloves garlic, 1 tbs chopped mint,*
*1 tbs chopped parsley, 1 red bell pepper, 1 tbs currants,*
*½ oz pine nuts, Freshly ground pepper, Salt,*
*Grease for the casserole dish, 1 tbs tomato paste*

Combine rice and stock, bring to a boil, and simmer over very low heat until all the liquid has been absorbed. In the meantime, cut caps off the tomatoes and hollow out carefully. Set aside seeds and juice. Place tomatoes on paper towels with the cut sides down. Peel and chop onions. In a pan, heat half the olive oil and brown onion. Squeeze garlic through a press and add to onion. Add interiors of tomatoes and bring to a boil. Stir in mint and parsley. Cut bell pepper in half, remove stem, seeds and interiors, and cut into small cubes and add to sauce. If sauce cooks down too much, add water and simmer for 5 minutes. Add currants and pine nuts. Stir in rice and season with salt and pepper.

Grease a casserole dish. Fill tomatoes three-quarters full with the rice mixture, arrange side by side in the casserole dish, and cover with the appropriate caps. Combine remaining oil and tomato paste and spread all around on the tomatoes. If you have any filling left over, add it to the casserole dish. Bake in an oven preheated to 350°F for about 30 minutes.

## Tomato Zucchini Boats

*4 medium zucchini, Salt, 1 cup tomatoes, 1 green onion,*
*2 tbs olive oil, ½ tsp chopped thyme or basil, 1 tbs balsamic vinegar,*
*Freshly ground pepper, 1 pinch sugar (optional),*
*2 ½ oz pine nuts, 7 tbs crème fraîche★,*
*3½ tbs crumbled blue cheese (e.g., Gorgonzola), 1 ½ tbs butter*

Clean zucchini, cut in half lengthwise, sprinkle with salt to draw out water, and let stand for 10 minutes. Then rinse, pat dry, and scrape out seeds with a spoon. Cut tomatoes in half, remove cores and seeds, and dice flesh. Clean green onion and cut into fine rings. In a pan, heat olive oil and briefly braise tomatoes and green onion. Add herbs and season with vinegar, salt, pepper, and sugar, if desired. Stir in pine nuts, crème fraîche, and blue cheese. Spoon mixture into the zucchini halves.

In a pan with a lid, melt butter. Place zucchini boats in the pan and brown. Reduce temperature, cover, and braise vegetables for 15 minutes. If the zucchini stick to the bottom, add a little water.

★ Crème fraîche is available in gourmet shops, or can be made by combining 1 cup whipping cream with 2 tbs buttermilk in a covered glass container at room temperature, about 70°F. Let stand for 8 to 24 hours, or until very thick.

🍅 You can also bake these in a 400°F oven for 15 minutes or use eggplant instead of zucchini.

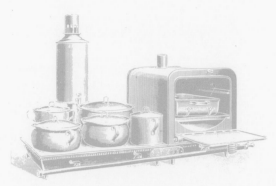

## Tomato Couscous

*1⅓ cups red and yellow cherry tomatoes (about 10½ oz),*
*4 tbs cold-pressed olive oil, 7 oz couscous, 1 cup hot water or vegetable stock,*
*1 tbs butter, 1 can white beans (about 15 ¼ oz), ½ cup feta cheese,*
*2 tsp chopped mint, Sea salt, Freshly ground black pepper*

Preheat oven to 425°F. Brush a baking dish with 1 tbs olive oil. Arrange tomatoes side by side in the dish and brush with another tablespoon of oil. Heat in the oven for about 5 minutes (the peel should blister slightly).

Pour couscous into a bowl and pour on water or stock. Add remaining olive oil, stir, and let stand for 5 minutes. Then fluff with a fork and pour into a fine-mesh strainer. Suspend the strainer over a pot of boiling water and steam couscous for 10-15 minutes. Then return to the bowl. Add butter and fold into the couscous with a fork until completely melted.

Pour beans into a colander and rinse. Crumble feta. Carefully mix beans and feta into couscous. Add half the mint. Season with sea salt and black pepper. Carefully fold in tomatoes, sprinkle dish with remaining mint, and serve warm as a light lunch.

🍅 If you prefer your tomatoes without the skins, peel the tomatoes after broiling.

# Vegetable Rice Pot

*1 cup long-grain rice, 1 onion, 2 tbs butter, 1 cup tomato juice,*
*1 cup vegetable stock, ½ cup broccoli, ½ cup cauliflower,*
*1 small red bell pepper, 1 small zucchini, ½ cup fresh mushrooms,*
*½ cup snow peas, 2 tbs olive oil, 2 cloves garlic,*
*1 cup cherry tomatoes, Salt,*
*Freshly ground pepper, Hungarian sweet paprika*

Pour rice into a strainer and rinse under running water until the water flows clear. Peel and dice onion. In a saucepan, heat 1 tbs butter and sauté rice and onion. Pour in tomato juice and stock and bring to a boil. Stir and cook over low heat for about 20 minutes (follow package instructions).

In the meantime, clean broccoli and cauliflower and divide into florets. Cut bell pepper in half, remove stem, seeds and interiors, and cut into bite-sized pieces. Clean and dice zucchini. Clean mushrooms (do not rinse) and cut into quarters. Clean snow peas and cut in half crosswise. In a pan with a lid, heat olive oil and remaining butter and briefly braise vegetables along with garlic squeezed through a press. Add tomatoes, stir, cover, and cook vegetables for up to 8 minutes until al dente. If the tomatoes don't yield enough juice, add a little water. Season liberally with salt, pepper, and paprika. Stir in rice and serve immediately.

## Stuffed Pancakes

*For the batter: 1 cup flour, 2 eggs, 1 pinch salt, No more than 2 cups milk*
*For the filling: 1 lb firm red tomatoes, 1 onion, 1 tsp butter,*
*1 tbs chopped basil, 1 dash dried oregano, Salt,*
*Freshly ground pepper, 10 slices bacon,*
*1 lb yellow tomatoes, 3 tbs flour or bread crumbs*
*Plus: Oil for frying*

For the batter: Sift flour into a bowl. Stir in eggs, salt, and milk. Cover and let stand for 30 minutes.

In the meantime, make the filling: Blanch red tomatoes, peel, remove cores, and chop. Peel onion and mince. In a pan, heat butter and sauté onions until translucent. Add chopped tomatoes and bring to a boil. Braise for several minutes and then put through a strainer. Season with basil, oregano, salt, and pepper. In a pan, render bacon until crispy. Remove and drain on paper towels.

In a small pan, heat oil and fry batter on both sides to form pancakes. Keep warm.

Remove cores from yellow tomatoes and cut into thick slices. Dredge in flour or bread crumbs and fry in the grease remaining in the pan until golden-brown on both sides, then remove.

Top half the pancakes with a thick layer of fried tomato slices. Place the other half on top. Pour on sauce and top with fried bacon.

If you don't like bacon, sprinkle pancakes with grated cheese. You can also brown them in the oven.

Instead of pancakes, make salty crêpes or Spanish tortillas and serve with filling and sauce.

## Tomato Mozzarella Omelet

The cardinal rules for a successful omelet are: Separate the eggs, do not add flour to the batter, and fry in a nonstick pan.

*5 eggs, 1/3 cup heavy cream, Salt, 1/2 bunch parsley,*
*1/2 cup mozzarella, 3 large meaty tomatoes,*
*1 1/2–3 tbs butter, Several stalks arugula, Lemon pepper*

Separate eggs. Beat egg yolks with cream and a little salt until foamy. Beat egg whites until stiff. Rinse parsley, pat dry, remove leaves from stems, and chop. Carefully fold egg whites and parsley into the egg cream. Remove cores from tomatoes and cut tomatoes and mozzarella into uniform slices.

Heat butter in 2 pans with lids. Pour half the batter into each pan and cook over medium heat until it sets slightly. Arrange cheese and tomato slices in a fan pattern on top of the omelets. Rinse several arugula leaves, pat dry, and scatter on top. Shake pan back and forth occasionally to keep the omelets from sticking. Cover and cook for 5 minutes. The finished omelets should be fully set but still moist and shiny. Slide onto plates, sprinkle with lemon pepper, and eat while hot.

## Tomato Potato Casserole

*2 1/4 lb firm tomatoes, 2 medium onions, 2 tbs oil,*
*4 tbs butter, Salt, Freshly ground pepper, 2 tbs grated Parmesan*

Peel potatoes, rinse, and cut into thin slices. Blanch tomatoes, peel, remove cores, and cut into thick slices. Peel and dice onions. In a pan, heat oil and braise onions until translucent. Pour onion grease into a casserole dish and layer potatoes and tomatoes on top. Top each layer with butter cut into bits and season with salt and pepper. Finish with a layer of tomatoes and sprinkle with Parmesan. Cover casserole dish with a lid (or aluminum foil) and bake in an oven preheated to 425°F for 60–70 minutes. This casserole is a perfect side dish with cutlets, fried fish filets, or hard-boiled eggs.

## Tomato Soufflé

*1 cup firm potatoes, Salt, 1 small onion, 3½ tbs cooked ham,*
*3 tbs butter, 2 tbs flour, 1 cup cold milk,*
*1 small can tomato paste, 3½ oz grated Gouda,*
*Freshly ground pepper, Juice of ½ lemon, 3 eggs,*
*5 tomatoes, Grease for the casserole dish*

Peel potatoes, rinse, cook in salted water, and let cool. Peel onion and dice onion and ham. In a saucepan, melt butter and briefly sweat onion and ham. Whisk together flour and milk, add tomato paste, and pour into the ham-onion mixture. Cook thoroughly for 5 minutes. Remove pan from heat and stir in grated cheese. Season with salt, pepper, and lemon juice. Separate eggs. Stir egg yolks into the sauce. Cut potatoes into slices and add. Beat egg whites until stiff and fold into the sauce. Blanch tomatoes, peel, cut into quarters, and remove cores and seeds. Grease a deep casserole dish and distribute tomato pieces inside. Pour in egg mixture. Important: Do not fill the casserole dish more than three-quarters full. Bake soufflé on the middle rack of an oven preheated to 350–400°F for about 35 minutes. Do not under any circumstances open the oven door while the soufflé is cooking (soufflés can't tolerate a draft and will collapse!). Serve immediately. Delicious with any sort of green salad.

## Tomato Eggplant Casserole

*3⅓ lb eggplant, Salt, Oil for frying, Grease for the baking dish,*
*½ cup Parmesan, 1 cup mozzarella,*
*1 recipe Classic Tomato Sauce (recipe on page 97),*
*4 tbs chopped basil*

Clean eggplant and slice lengthwise. Arrange slices on paper towels and sprinkle with salt to draw out the bitter juices. Then rinse and pat dry. In a pan, heat oil and sauté eggplant slices on both sides until golden-brown.

Grease a baking dish and fill with alternating layers of eggplant, grated Parmesan, and sliced mozzarella until all the ingredients have been used. Top each layer with tomato sauce and sprinkle with basil. Finish with a layer of cheese. Bake in an oven preheated to 350°F for 40 minutes.

You can use this same recipe to prepare a zucchini casserole. Simply replace eggplant with the same amount of zucchini.

## Tomato Noodle Casserole

*1 cup penne rigate, Salt, 2 tbs oil, 7 oz cooked ham,*
*3⅓ cups plum tomatoes, 1 bunch chives, 4 eggs,*
*1 cup heavy cream, Freshly ground pepper,*
*Grease for the casserole dish, 7 oz mozzarella, 3 tbs butter*

Following the package instructions, cook penne in a large amount of salted water to which oil has been added, until al dente. Then drain. Dice ham. Blanch tomatoes, peel, remove cores, and slice. Rinse chives, pat dry, and chop. Whisk together eggs, cream, salt, and pepper.

Grease a casserole dish and fill with layers of tomatoes, chives, penne, and ham. Finish with a layer of tomatoes. Pour on egg cream. Cut mozzarella into thin slices and arrange in a fan pattern on top. Top with butter cut into bits and bake in an oven preheated to 400°F for about 45 minutes. Delicious with a fresh green salad.

## Vegetable Casserole

*1 lb tomatoes, 2 onions, 7 oz zucchini, Grease for the casserole dish,*
*3½ oz thinly sliced smoked ham, Salt, Freshly ground black pepper,*
*1 clove garlic, 1 tbs oil, 1 tbs dried marjoram,*
*⅓ cup grated Emmenthaler, 2 tbs bread crumbs*

Remove cores from tomatoes and cut into quarters or slice. Peel onions and cut into rings. Clean zucchini and cut into slices ½-inch thick. Grease a casserole dish and fill with alternating layers of tomatoes, onions, zucchini, and ham, finishing with a layer of tomatoes. Season each tomato layer with salt and pepper. Peel garlic, squeeze through a press, and mix with oil and marjoram. Drizzle mixture over the casserole. Sprinkle the top layer with cheese and bread crumbs. Bake in an oven preheated to 400°F for about 15 minutes.

🍅 You can also sauté zucchini slices on both sides until golden-brown before adding them to the casserole.

# Tomato Cheese Cannelloni

*1 lb mild cheese (e.g., young Gouda), 16 cannelloni,*
*2¼ lb firm tomatoes, 1 cup onions, 2 cloves garlic,*
*2 tbs oil, Salt, Freshly ground black pepper, A little sugar,*
*½ cup red wine, 1 stalk rosemary,*
*1 tbs tomato paste, Butter for the casserole dish*

Cut cheese into narrow slices the same length as the cannelloni and place them inside. Blanch tomatoes, peel, remove cores, and dice. Peel onions and garlic and chop. In a pan, heat oil and sweat onions and garlic. Add tomatoes and season with salt, pepper, and sugar. Stir in red wine. Rinse rosemary stalk and add. Simmer for 10 minutes, then add tomato paste and remove rosemary. Butter a casserole dish, arrange cannelloni inside, and pour sauce over the top. Bake in an oven preheated to 400°F for 45 minutes.

For a change, fill the cannelloni with seasoned ricotta or feta and fresh chopped herbs.

## Turkish Casserole

*For the casserole: 1 lb lean ground lamb, 3 large onions,
2 cloves garlic, Salt, 2 tbs Hungarian sweet paprika,
4 large beefsteak tomatoes, 1 lb potatoes, ½ bunch thyme,
½ bunch chervil, ½ cup meat stock
For the sauce: 2¼ cups Turkish yogurt (available at gourmet shops,
or substitute full-fat, high-quality plain or Greek yogurt),
Several dashes lemon juice, Salt, Freshly ground pepper,
1 pinch sugar, 1 tsp tomato paste
Plus: Clarified butter and butter for frying,
Grease for the casserole dish*

For the casserole: Place ground lamb in a bowl. Peel onions and garlic, chop finely, and add to meat. Season with salt and paprika. Blanch tomatoes, peel, remove cores, and chop. In a pan, heat clarified butter and brown seasoned ground meat until crumbly. Add tomatoes and simmer for 5 minutes.

Peel potatoes, rinse, and cut into thin slices. In a pan, heat butter and brown potato slices. Season with salt. Grease a casserole dish, fill with meat-tomato mixture, and smooth out the surface. Layer potatoes on top. Rinse herbs, pat dry, remove leaves, and chop. Add to stock and pour over potatoes. Bake in an oven preheated to 350–400°F for about 1 hour.

In the meantime, make the sauce: Combine yogurt and lemon juice and season to taste with salt, pepper, sugar, and tomato paste. Serve this cold yogurt sauce with the casserole.

If desired, you can sprinkle the casserole with crumbled feta 20 minutes before it's done cooking.

## Tomato Plaki

Imported from Turkey and the Balkans, this dish is highly valued in Bulgaria and Greece. It is served both warm and cold, with roast lamb or grilled fish, but is often simply prepared as a stew.

*3⅓ cups tomatoes, 4 large onions, 1-2 cloves garlic,*
*1 bunch parsley or dill, 8 pitted black olives,*
*Grease for the casserole dish, 4 tbs sunflower oil,*
*Juice of 1 lemon, Salt, Freshly ground pepper, 1 pinch sugar*

Blanch tomatoes, peel, remove cores, and slice. Peel onions and cut into rings. Peel garlic and mince. Rinse parsley or dill, pat dry, remove leaves from stems, and chop. Cut olives into thin slices.

Grease a casserole dish with a lid. Combine sunflower oil, lemon juice, garlic, and parsley or dill. In the casserole dish, layer tomatoes, onions, and olives, drizzling each layer with herb oil, and seasoning with salt, pepper, and a little sugar. Finish with a layer of tomatoes. Seal casserole dish tightly and bake on the lowest rack of an oven preheated to 425°F for about 25 minutes.

Try making this in the Greek style: Include layers of raw, firm fish fillets in the casserole before baking it in the oven. Naturally, this dish is eaten warm.

# Moussaka

Moussaka is a Greek culinary classic. Although I have only heard this once, from a person in Greece, "genuine Moussaka should not contain potatoes." However, I enjoy this particular recipe with potatoes.

*Serves 6:*
*1 lb eggplant, Salt, 1 lb potatoes, 1 cup olive oil,*
*Freshly ground pepper, ½ tsp dried rosemary needles,*
*2¼ lb ground lamb, 1 lb ground meat (half beef, half pork),*
*1 cup onions, 3 cloves garlic, 1 tsp fresh chopped thyme,*
*1 tsp fresh chopped sage, 2¼ lb large meaty tomatoes,*
*Paprika, 6 eggs, 1 cup heavy cream*

Clean eggplant and cut into slices ¼-inch thick. Spread out on paper towels and sprinkle with salt. Draw out water for 10 minutes and then pat dry. Peel potatoes, rinse, and cook in salted water until half done. Drain, let cool, and cut into thin slices. Brush a little olive oil onto a large casserole dish. Fill with potato slices and season with salt, pepper, and rosemary.

Combine the different types of ground meat. Peel onions and garlic and dice finely. In a pan, heat a little olive oil and sauté meat with onions and garlic until crumbly. Season with salt, pepper, and chopped herbs. Spoon meat mixture onto the potatoes in the casserole dish. Blanch tomatoes, peel, cut into quarters, and remove seeds and cores. In the remaining olive oil, briefly sauté eggplant slices on both sides. Drain on paper towels. Arrange alternating rows of eggplant and tomato in an overlapping pattern on top of the meat. Season with salt, pepper, and paprika.

Whisk together eggs and cream and pour over the casserole. Bake in an oven preheated to 400°F for 30–40 minutes.

 You can also top the casserole with grated Greek cheese (e.g., Kefalotiri) or Parmesan and tomato slices.

 In the classic version of Moussaka, a béchamel sauce is poured over the top instead of the egg cream.

# MEAT DISHES

## Hungarian Goulash

This famous Eastern Hungarian Puszta dish, which will warm you body and soul, must be spicy, thick, and creamy.

*1 lb onions, 2¼ lb beef, 3½ tbs lard,*
*Salt, Freshly ground pepper, 1 tsp caraway,*
*Hungarian hot paprika, 1 cup red wine, 2 cups stock,*
*2 carrots, 3⅓ cups potatoes, 1 lb red bell peppers,*
*1 lb beefsteak tomatoes, 1 tbs tomato paste, 2–3 drops Tabasco sauce*

Peel onions and dice coarsely. Cut beef into large cubes. In a roasting pan, heat lard and sear beef cubes on all sides. Add onions and roast briefly. Season with salt, pepper, caraway, and paprika. Add wine and half the stock, cover, and stew meat for about 1 hour. From time to time, replace the liquid that is boiled away with the remaining stock.

In the meantime, prepare the vegetables. Peel carrots and cut into small cubes. Peel potatoes and cut into large cubes. Cut bell peppers in half, remove stems, seeds and interiors, and dice. After 1 hour, add carrots, potatoes and peppers to the meat, and cook for another 45–60 minutes. In the meantime, blanch tomatoes, peel, and remove cores and seeds, setting aside any juice. Dice flesh coarsely and 10 minutes before the goulash is done cooking, stir in tomatoes, the juice you saved, tomato paste, and Tabasco. If there isn't enough liquid, add water. Although the goulash should not have a lot of sauce, it must always stew in liquid. Serve with potato dumplings or alone with crispy rolls.

🌶 You can increase the spiciness of this dish, for example, by adding more Tabasco or paprika. If desired, roast 1 small, chopped chile pepper along with the other vegetables.

## Baked Tenderloin Steaks

*4 beef tenderloin steaks (5–7 oz each), Freshly ground pepper,*
*4 tbs oil, 4 slices raw ham, 4 tomatoes,*
*4 slices Emmenthaler or Gouda, A little paprika*

Season steaks with pepper and brush with 1 tbs oil. Let stand for 1 hour, then heat remaining oil in a pan, and fry steaks for 3 minutes on each side. Transfer to a casserole dish and cover with ham. Remove cores from tomatoes and slice. Arrange slices on the meat in an overlapping pattern and top with cheese.

Bake in an oven preheated to 350–400°F until the cheese has melted. Dust with paprika and serve immediately with freshly toasted bread or fried potatoes.

## Ossobuco

*4 slices veal shank (7 oz each), Salt, Freshly ground pepper,*
*Flour for dredging, 4 tbs olive oil, 3 tbs balsamic vinegar,*
*½ cup red wine, ½ cup white wine, 2 cups stock,*
*2 cloves garlic, 1 cup beefsteak tomatoes,*
*3 green onions, 1 tbs tomato paste, Several sage leaves*

Rinse meat, pat dry, and season with salt and pepper. Dredge in flour. In a pan, heat oil and brown veal shank slices on both sides for a total of 7 minutes. Pour in vinegar, wine, and stock. Cover and roast for 1 hour.

In the meantime, peel and dice garlic. Blanch tomatoes, cut into quarters, and remove seeds and cores. Clean green onions and cut diagonally into pieces ½-inch long. Add vegetables to meat 10 minutes before it is done cooking. Stir in tomato paste and season to taste with salt and pepper. Rinse sage leaves, pat dry, and use to garnish Ossobuco. Serve with risotto.

 The garnish is especially elegant if you deep-fry the sage beforehand.

 Variation: You can turn this dish into Ossobuco alla Milanese by roasting 1 finely chopped carrot and 1 stalk celery along with vegetables. Season to taste with grated peel from 1 organic lemon.

## English-Style Meatballs

*For the meatballs: 1½ lb ground meat (half beef, half pork),*
*Salt, Freshly ground pepper, 2 eggs, 1 onion, 2 tbs bread crumbs,*
*1 tbs green peppercorns*
*For each meatball: ½ dried tomato in oil,*
*1 cheese cube (e.g., pecorino, cheddar, etc.), 1 slice bacon, 2 tbs sunflower oil*
*For the sauce: 1 recipe Classic Tomato Sauce (recipe on page 97,*
*but prepared with mint instead of basil!)*

Place ground meat in a bowl and season with salt and pepper. Peel onion and chop finely. Add eggs, onion, bread crumbs, and green peppercorns to meat and knead thoroughly. Wet your hands and shape meat into small balls. Drain dried tomatoes and cut in half lengthwise. Wrap 1 cube cheese in each dried-tomato half and press into a meatball, carefully closing the meat around it. Then wrap each meatball in 1 slice bacon and secure with a toothpick. In a pan, heat oil and fry meatballs on all sides until crispy. In the meantime, prepare tomato sauce according to the recipe and serve with the meatballs.

 Serve cooled meatballs as a party snack with Sicilian-Style Pesto Rosso (recipe on page 96). The toothpicks serve as "handles" for this finger food.

## Apulian Lamb Pot

*2¼ lb tender lean lamb (e.g., from the shoulder or leg),*
*Salt, Freshly ground black pepper, 1½ tbs lard or clarified butter,*
*1 clove garlic, 1 stalk rosemary, 1 bunch thyme, 2 bay leaves,*
*2 cups dry red wine, 1 lb green bell peppers,*
*1 cup small onions, 1 cup cherry tomatoes*

Cut lamb into large cubes and season with salt and pepper. In a roasting pan, heat lard and sear meat on all sides. Peel garlic and squeeze through a press. Rinse herbs and pat dry. Strip thyme leaves from stems and leave rosemary whole. Add herbs, garlic, bay leaves, and red wine to meat and roast for 30 minutes. Cut bell peppers in half, remove stems, seeds and interiors, and cut into bite-sized pieces. Peel onions. After 30 minutes, add peppers and onions to meat and roast for an additional 30 minutes. Blanch tomatoes, peel, remove cores, and add to lamb 10 minutes before it's done cooking. Then remove bay leaves and rosemary. This dish from Apulia in Southern Italy goes with rice, olives and a fresh salad, or else simply with fresh country bread.

# Tomato Bredie

A Bredie is a stew and is practically the national dish of South Africa. The original Bredie was imported by the Boers from their native Holland. It was often made without potatoes and then served with mashed potatoes or rice, for example.

*2 onions, 1 lb lamb chops, Salt, Freshly ground pepper,*
*Hungarian hot paprika, 1 lb tomatoes,*
*1 small, fresh red chile pepper, 3½ tbs clarified butter or oil,*
*1 cup meat stock, 1 tsp sugar or honey*

Peel onions and cut into rings. Season lamb chops with salt, pepper, and paprika. Blanch tomatoes, peel, remove cores, and slice. Slit open chile pepper, remove stem, seeds and interiors, and dice very finely.

In a pan, heat half the clarified butter or oil and briefly sauté meat on both sides. In a pot, heat remaining butter or oil, and braise onions until translucent. Place lamb chops on top and cover these with a layer of tomato slices. Sprinkle with chile pepper. Dissolve sugar or honey in hot stock, pour over meat, season with salt and pepper, and cook over low heat for 30 minutes.

## Chicken Breast à la Niçoise

*4 chicken breast fillets, Salt, Freshly ground pepper,*
*Paprika, 2 onions, 1 lb tomatoes, 10–15 pitted black olives,*
*3–4 cloves garlic, 4 tbs olive oil, 1 stalk thyme,*
*2 bay leaves, 1 tbs tomato paste, 1 cup dry white wine*

Season chicken with salt, pepper, and paprika. Peel onions and cut into rings. Blanch tomatoes, peel, cut into quarters, and remove cores. Cut olives in half. Peel garlic and slice finely.

In a pan with a lid, heat olive oil, brown meat on both sides, and remove. Briefly brown onions in the same grease, then add garlic, tomatoes, and olives. Rinse thyme and bay leaves and add. Stir in tomato paste and white wine. Bring to a boil, add chicken breast fillets, cover, and braise gently for 20 minutes. Remove thyme and bay leaves. Transfer to a deep platter.

🍅 You can also arrange the fillets in a buttered casserole dish with vegetables all around, sprinkle with grated cheese, and bake in an oven preheated to 400°F for 30 minutes.

## Greek Tomato Chicken

*2 leeks, 3⅓ cups vine tomatoes, 1 organic orange,*
*4 chicken breast fillets, Salt, Freshly ground pepper,*
*1 tbs oil, 1 cup chicken stock, 7 oz dried apricots,*
*3½ tbs raisins, ½ tsp dried oregano, 2½ oz pine nuts*

Clean leak and cut into pieces 1-inch long. Blanch tomatoes, peel, cut into quarters, and remove seeds and cores. Grate peel from the orange and squeeze out juice.

Rinse chicken breast fillets, pat dry, and season with salt and pepper. In a sauté pan, heat oil and brown fillets on both sides. Remove and keep warm. Stir orange juice and stock into pan residues. Add leeks, tomatoes, orange peel, apricots and raisins, and cook uncovered for 10 minutes. Season with salt, pepper and oregano, and place chicken fillets on top. Then cover and braise for another 10 minutes. Remove pan from heat and let stand for 5 minutes. Do not remove the lid!

In an ungreased pan, toast pine nuts. Sprinkle over tomato chicken and serve with boiled or roasted potatoes.

🍅 If desired, sprinkle tomatoes with sage leaves and then top with cheese.

# FISH & SEAFOOD DISHES

## Tomato Carp Ragout

*1 lb beefsteak tomatoes, 1 cup cherry tomatoes,*
*²/₃ cup onions, 1 red bell pepper, 2 tbs lard, 3 oz diced bacon,*
*1–1½ cups vegetable stock, 1 tsp tomato paste,*
*Salt, Freshly ground pepper, 1 lb carp fillets, 2–3 tbs lemon juice,*
*7 tbs sour cream or crème fraîche★ (about 3½ oz),*
*2 tbs white wine, 3 stalks parsley*

Blanch beefsteak and cherry tomatoes, peel, and remove cores. Dice beefsteak tomatoes and leave cherry tomatoes whole. Peel onions and chop coarsely. Cut bell pepper in half, remove stem, seeds and interiors, and cut into bite-sized pieces. In a saucepan, heat lard and briefly brown diced bacon. Add beefsteak tomatoes, onions and bell pepper, and sauté without browning. Pour in stock, stir in tomato paste, and season with salt and pepper. Simmer for 10 minutes.

In the meantime, rinse fish, pat dry, cut into large pieces, and drizzle with lemon juice. Marinate for 10 minutes. Combine sour cream or crème fraîche with wine and fold into the tomato mixture. Place fish and cherry tomatoes on top and let stand for another 5-10 minutes, but stop simmering. Stir carefully before serving. Rinse parsley, pat dry, remove leaves from stems, chop, and sprinkle a thick layer onto the ragout. Goes with rice or potatoes boiled with or without their skins.

★ Crème fraîche is available in gourmet shops, or can be made by combining 1 cup whipping cream with 2 tbs buttermilk in a covered glass container at room temperature, about 70°F. Let stand for 8 to 24 hours, or until very thick.

# Fish Fillets in Foil

*1 lb firm plum tomatoes, 1 yellow bell pepper, 2 cloves garlic,*
*1 bunch basil, 1½ lb firm fish fillets (e.g., pollack, cod, tuna),*
*1 tbs lemon juice, Salt, Freshly ground pepper,*
*3 ½ tbs sliced almonds, 4 tbs olive oil*

Blanch tomatoes, peel, cut into quarters, and remove cores. Cut bell pepper in half, remove stem, seeds and interiors, and cut into strips. Peel garlic and slice finely. Rinse basil, pat dry, remove leaves from stems, and cut into strips.

Form a large sheet of extra-strength aluminum foil into a bowl with the shiny side inward, leaving enough margin around the edges so you can close the foil over the top. Combine tomatoes, bell pepper, garlic and basil, and transfer to this bowl.

Rinse fish fillets, pat dry, rub with lemon juice, season with salt and pepper, and place on top of the vegetables. In an ungreased pan, toast sliced almonds until golden-brown. Scatter over the fish. Drizzle with oil and seal the foil. Bake in an oven preheated to 425°F for 20 minutes, then remove. Open foil and transfer fish and vegetables to a preheated platter. Goes with risotto.

🍅 You can also cook the fish in individual foil packages that each person opens on his or her plate.

# Baked Salt Cod

Every year for four centuries, the Portuguese fishing fleet has sailed from Lisbon to the fishing grounds off the coast of Newfoundland. Here, fishermen catch the prized cod (bacalhau) and immediately salt it on the spot. After six months of fishing, they return to Portugal where the fish is dried in the sun at processing plants. The dried cod is known as salt cod and, prepared in a variety of ways, is a delicacy of Portuguese cuisine.

*1½ lb salt cod (4 slices), 2 cups milk, 3 tsp olive oil,*
*4 tomatoes, 12 thick slices smoked ham (⅛-inch slices),*
*2 hard-boiled eggs, 4 tbs pitted black olives, 2 tsp chopped parsley*

On the previous day, place fish in a bowl, cover with cold water, and soak for 12 hours, changing water several times. On the next day, rinse under running water, pat dry, and use a knife to remove skin and bones. Arrange fish slices side by side in a casserole dish.

Heat milk but do not allow to boil. Pour over fish and let stand for 1 hour. Drain and discard milk. Preheat oven to 350°F. Drizzle fish with oil and bake in the oven for 15 minutes. If necessary, brush once with oil. Remove cores from tomatoes and slice. Arrange ham and tomato slices on the fish in a fish-scale pattern. Drizzle with any fish gravy that accumulated. Bake in the oven for another 5 minutes. Peel eggs. Put egg yolks through a strainer. Chop olives or cut into quarters. Combine egg yolks, olives and parsley, and sprinkle over the dish. If you want, you can finely chop the egg whites and mix them with the other sprinkled ingredients. Otherwise, find another use them. Serve in the casserole dish.

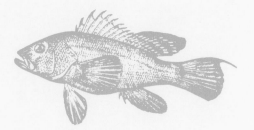

# Rockfish in a Tomato Blanket

*4 rockfish fillets (e.g., Pacific snapper), Lemon juice,*
*Salt, Freshly ground pepper, 4 tbs flour, 1 egg,*
*4 tbs bread crumbs, 6-8 beefsteak tomatoes, 1 red onion,*
*Grease for frying, 12 basil leaves, 2 tbs cold-pressed olive oil*

Rinse fish fillets, pat dry, drizzle with lemon juice, and marinate for 10 minutes. Then pat dry and season with salt and pepper. Dredge fillets one at a time in flour, then whisked egg, and then bread crumbs.

Blanch tomatoes, peel, cut in half, and remove cores and seeds. Peel and chop onion. In a pan, heat grease, briefly braise tomatoes, and then remove. Brown onions in the same grease and keep both vegetables warm. Rinse basil and pat dry.

In fresh grease, brown fish fillets on both sides. On a preheated platter, arrange tomato halves and onions. Sprinkle with half the basil leaves and place fish on top. Cover with remaining tomatoes and basil leaves and drizzle with olive oil. Goes with basmati rice.

## Spanish-Style Hake Fillets with Tomato Almond Sauce

*For the fish: 2¼ lb hake fillets (may substitute haddock or cod),*
*1 tsp salt, 3 tsp lemon juice*
*For the sauce: 2 onions, 2 cloves garlic, 1 lb plum tomatoes,*
*4 tbs cold-pressed olive oil, 3 tbs ground almonds,*
*1 slice stale white bread, 1 tsp lemon juice, 1 tsp salt, ½ cup fish stock*
*Plus: Slivered almonds and chopped parsley for garnish*

For the fish: Bring 6 cups salted water with lemon juice to a boil. Rinse fillets and simmer in the water for 10 minutes until done. Do not boil!

In the meantime, prepare the sauce: Peel onions and garlic and chop finely. Blanch tomatoes, peel, remove seeds and cores, and dice finely. In a pan, heat oil and braise onions and garlic, while stirring until translucent. Add almonds. Remove crust from bread and crumble bread into the pan. Add tomatoes and simmer uncovered so that as much liquid is boiled away as possible. Season to taste with lemon juice and salt. Stir in fish stock.

Transfer fish fillets to a preheated platter and pour on sauce. Serve sprinkled with a thick layer of slivered almonds and parsley.

🍅 You can also toast the slivered almonds in an ungreased pan until golden-brown.

## Mussels in Tomato Sauce

This dish comes from Calabria, where it is served with garlic bread or ciabatta drizzled with olive oil.

*3 ½ lb fresh mussels, 1 bunch soup greens (combination carrot,*
*celery, parsnip, turnip, dill, leek, and parsley with total amounts to 1 ½ lb),*
*2 stalks celery, 2 onions, ½ cup olive oil, 4 bay leaves,*
*1 bunch thyme, 1 cup dry white wine,*
*2 ¼ lb beefsteak tomatoes (may substitute 1 large can peeled tomatoes),*
*3 fresh chile peppers, Salt (optional)*

Scrub mussels under running water, discarding any that are open or broken. De-beard. Clean, peel, and chop soup greens as appropriate. Peel and dice onions.

In a large pot, heat oil and briefly braise prepared vegetables. Add bay leaves and entire bundle of thyme. Pour in wine and simmer for 10 minutes. In the meantime, blanch tomatoes, peel, cut into quarters, and remove cores (drain canned tomatoes and chop into smaller pieces). Slit open chile peppers, remove stems, seeds and interiors, and mince.

Add tomatoes, chile peppers, and mussels to the vegetables in the pot. Stir well, cover, and simmer for 6–8 minutes. Carefully stir once more. Remove and discard any mussels that have not opened. Add salt to liquid, if desired. Remove thyme bundle and bay leaves. Transfer dish to a preheated soup terrine or individual soup plates.

Here's how to eat mussels: Use an empty shell as tweezers to remove the meat, then spoon on the liquid.

## Scallops

Bay scallops live along the Atlantic and Mediterranean coasts and are among the tastiest of shellfish.

Pilgrims on their way to Santiago de Compostela, Spain, used the convex, empty shells as drinking vessels that they wore on their hats as a sign of their pilgrimage. Even today, scallop shells serve as markers all along the old pilgrim route, known as the "Way of Saint James."

Unfortunately, fresh bay scallops are less plentiful and therefore more expensive than the larger, chewier, yet still sweet sea scallops. The sweeter, more succulent bay scallops are also available frozen or canned. Sea scallops may also be used in this recipe.

*1 1/2 lb shucked scallop meat (muscle and roe),*
*4 beefsteak tomatoes, 2 stalks basil, 7 tbs butter,*
*Salt, Freshly ground pepper, Chopped dill for garnish*

Lay fresh scallops on a hot burner. When they open, pull up the top half and remove the meat. Remove the black innards and the "skirt." Drain canned scallop meat. Blanch tomatoes, peel, remove seeds and cores, and dice. Rinse basil, pat dry, remove leaves from stems, and cut into strips.

In a pan, heat butter until foamy and add scallop meat. Season with salt and pepper. Sauté briefly on both sides but be careful not to fry them for too long or they'll dry out! Remove and keep in a warm place. Toss tomatoes and basil in the butter. Season with salt and pepper and pour over the scallops. Serve garnished with dill.

## Canary Island Scampi

On the Canary Islands, scampi are served in the same way as scallops (see recipe above) after preparing them as follows: Devein, briefly marinate the meat with lemon juice, and then proceed as described above. You can also fry four small, chopped garlic cloves together with the scampi.

# DIPS & SAUCES

## Tomato Marinade

Tomato marinade is suitable for marinating steaks and fish fillets on the barbeque, usually for 1–2 hours, or as a dressing for a chicory, head lettuce, or mâche salad. It also tastes great with rice and pasta dishes and as a dressing for poultry salad.

*1 clove garlic, 3 tbs tomato paste, 1 tbs orange juice,*
*3 tbs oil, 3 tbs ketchup (recipe on page 106), 1 tbs lemon juice,*
*7 oz sour cream, Salt, Freshly ground pepper,*
*Oregano, 2 dashes Tabasco sauce*

Peel garlic and squeeze through a press, and whisk together with tomato juice, orange juice, oil, ketchup, lemon juice, and sour cream. Season with salt, pepper, oregano, and Tabasco. If you're marinating for grilling, turn the meat or fish after 1 hour. Brush with marinade several times while grilling.

## Tomato Dressing I

*2¼ lb ripe beefsteak tomatoes, 1 clove garlic,*
*1 shallot, 2 tbs cold-pressed olive oil, Several dashes lemon juice,*
*Salt, Freshly ground pepper, 1 pinch sugar*

Blanch tomatoes, peel, cut in half, and remove cores and stems, saving any juice. Dice flesh finely. Peel and mince garlic and shallot. Mix all these ingredients with olive oil and lemon juice. Season liberally with salt, pepper, and sugar. If necessary, stretch dressing with the tomato juice you saved. Serve with toasted white bread, or together with grated Parmesan as a sauce for pasta dishes.

🍅 The dressing will be even better if you place the tomatoes in the sun for 2 hours before preparation. This will allow their delicious aroma to unfold.

## Tomato Dressing II

Refine the Tomato Dressing I as follows and serve with warm asparagus, sautéed zucchini slices, or fried fish filet.

*1 recipe Tomato Dressing I (recipe above), 2 hard-boiled eggs,*
*1 tbs capers or green peppercorns, 1 tbs pink peppercorns,*
*1 large cup fresh chopped herbs (e.g., dill, parsley,*
*chives, thyme, lemon balm, basil)*

Prepare Tomato Dressing I as described in the recipe above. Peel eggs and chop. Stir eggs, capers, pepper and herbs into relish, and pour over warm vegetables or fish. Let marinate briefly.

## Mojo Rojo

It's impossible to imagine the cuisine of Mallorca and the Canary Islands without this sauce. Along with potatoes in a salt crust, it is an integral part of the midday snack of rural cuisine.

*1 fresh chile pepper, 2 small bell peppers, 1 lb tomatoes,*
*2 cloves garlic, 1 slice stale whole-wheat bread,*
*2 tbs cold-pressed olive oil, 1 tsp balsamic vinegar,*
*½ tsp cumin, ½ tsp Hungarian hot paprika,*
*½ tsp oregano, Salt, Freshly ground pepper*

Cut chile pepper and bell pepper in half, remove stems, seeds and interiors, and dice. Blanch tomatoes, peel, cut into quarters, and remove seeds and cores, saving any juice. Combine chile pepper, bell pepper, tomato flesh, and tomato juice in a blender and briefly pre-blend. Peel garlic and chop coarsely. Remove crust from bread and crumble. Add garlic, bread, olive oil, vinegar, and seasonings to the blender and purée until you have a smooth paste. Add seasoning to taste. Pour into a screw-top jar and cover surface with olive oil. Sauce keeps in the refrigerator for several days.

## Salsa Verde

Salsa Verde, the green tomato sauce from Mexico, is traditionally served with tortilla chips and cooked meat. But try it sometime heated and poured over hot, chopped, and fried chicken meat!

*10½ oz fresh green tomatoes (or canned), 1 onion,*
*½ clove garlic, 3 stalks parsley, 1 tsp chopped chile pepper,*
*½ tsp salt, Freshly ground black pepper*

Cook green tomatoes in very little water until tender and put through a strainer. Peel onion and garlic. Rinse parsley, pat dry, and remove leaves from stems. Purée all ingredients in a blender, including chile pepper, and season with salt and pepper.

## Sicilian-Style Pesto Rosso

Tomato pesto is delicious with any type of pasta dish, on toast, or as garnish on tomato soup.

*2 cloves garlic, 1 bunch basil, 8 dried tomatoes in oil,*
*2 tbs grated Parmesan, 2½ oz pine nuts or blanched almonds,*
*7 tbs cold-pressed olive oil, Sea salt*

Peel garlic. Rinse basil, pat dry, and remove leaves. Drain tomatoes. Combine garlic, basil, tomatoes, Parmesan and pine nuts or almonds in a blender, and purée, while gradually adding a thin stream of olive oil. Season with salt. Pour into a screw-top jar, cover surface with olive oil, and seal well. Pesto keeps in the refrigerator for 1–2 weeks, or you can freeze it.

## Spicy North African Seasoning Sauce

*1 lb tomatoes, 4 cloves garlic, 2 stalks mint,*
*5 stalks cilantro, 3 tbs red chile peppers,*
*½ tsp each of caraway seeds, cumin, and coriander*
*seeds, 1 cup defatted stock, 1 tbs lemon juice,*
*6 tbs cold-pressed olive oil, Salt, Sugar*

Blanch tomatoes, peel, remove cores and seeds, and chop finely. Peel and chop garlic. Rinse mint and cilantro, pat dry, remove leaves from stems, and chop. Cut chile peppers in half, remove seeds and interiors, and dice finely. In an ungreased pan, toast caraway seeds, cumin, and coriander seeds until they give off an aroma, then crush in a mortar. Combine spices with all other ingredients and let stand for 10 minutes, adding seasoning if desired. Let sauce marinate overnight. Keeps 1–2 weeks in the refrigerator. You can serve it with grilled fish or meat, tortilla chips, or boiled potatoes. You can also use it to season other sauces.

🍅 In Turkey, they also add 1 dash cinnamon and 2 tbs dried barberry. If you find that it's too sour, add a little sugar.

## Classic Tomato Sauce

It is said that a good cook is known by his or her sauces. There's something to that! It's the sauce that gives many dishes their pep. This tomato sauce should be cooked slowly while uncovered. Stir it occasionally to help the excess liquid boil away. If you boil it too much, the sauce becomes hard to digest. Don't season it until the very end. You can use this tomato sauce as a pizza topping and with pasta dishes, gnocchi, shrimp, and fish.

*2¼ lb beefsteak tomatoes, 3½ tbs shallots,*
*1 clove garlic, 4 tbs cold-pressed olive oil, 1 tsp sugar,*
*Salt, Freshly ground pepper, 3 tbs chopped basil leaves*

Blanch tomatoes, peel, remove cores, and dice. Peel and chop shallots and garlic. In a pot, heat olive oil and briefly sweat shallots and garlic. Sprinkle with sugar. Continue braising and stirring until the sugar has melted. Add tomatoes. Gently simmer uncovered until the diced tomatoes disintegrate. Season with salt and pepper. If desired, purée or put through a strainer. Stir in half the basil. Sprinkle the rest over the sauce just before serving.

🍅 With pasta dishes, serve with shaved Parmesan or pecorino.

🍅 You can also add 1–2 tsp tomato paste or chopped tomatoes from a slim-line carton to this sauce and season with Hungarian sweet paprika.

## Tomato Ham Sauce

*2 onions, 4 slices smoked ham, 4 beefsteak tomatoes,*
*1½ tbs butter, 7 oz herb cream cheese,*
*1 tbs peppercorns (green or pink, as desired)*

Peel and dice onions. Dice ham. Blanch tomatoes, peel, remove cores, and chop finely. In a pot, melt butter and braise onions and ham. Add tomatoes and simmer uncovered for 5 minutes. If necessary, add a little water, then stir in cream cheese and peppercorns, and briefly bring to a boil. Serve sauce with pasta or rice.

## Sauce Napoletana

*1 lb plum tomatoes, 1 large onion, 3½ tbs cooked ham,*
*2–3 tbs olive oil, 2 cups meat stock, Salt, Freshly ground pepper,*
*1 tsp Hungarian hot paprika, 1 pinch dried oregano,*
*1 pinch sugar, 2 stalks Italian parsley*

Blanch tomatoes, peel, remove cores, and dice. Peel and chop onion. Dice ham. In a pot, heat olive oil and briefly sweat onion and ham. Add tomatoes and bring to a boil. Pour in meat stock and simmer uncovered for 15 minutes. When the tomatoes have disintegrated, stir sauce thoroughly and season with salt, pepper, paprika, oregano, and sugar. Rinse parsley, pat dry, remove leaves from stems, chop, and stir into sauce at the last moment.

🍅 Replace half the meat stock with hard cider (apple wine) and enrich the sauce with 1–2 tbs crème fraîche, which is available in gourmet shops, or can be made by combining 1 cup whipping cream with 2 tbs buttermilk in a covered, glass container at room temperature, about 70°F. Let stand for 8 to 24 hours, or until very thick.

🍅 If you leave out the ham and parsley and let the sauce boil down and thicken, you can use it as a base for a pizza sauce.

## Bolognese Sauce

*1 large onion, ½ lb ground meat (half beef, half pork),*
*1 large carrot, 1 green bell pepper, 1 tbs olive oil, 1 lb plum tomatoes,*
*½ cup meat stock, 1 tbs tomato paste, 2 tbs cream cheese,*
*Salt, Freshly ground pepper, Hungarian hot paprika, ½ tsp dried rosemary,*
*½ tsp dried thyme, 1 tbs green peppercorns (optional)*

Peel and dice onion and knead into ground meat. Clean carrot and dice very finely. Cut bell pepper in half, remove stem, seeds and interiors, and dice very finely. In a wide pan, heat olive oil and brown meat until crumbly. Add prepared vegetables and sauté briefly. In the meantime, blanch tomatoes, peel, remove cores, and dice. Add to meat. Pour in stock and cook thoroughly. Then stir in tomato paste and cream cheese until thick and creamy. Season sauce with salt, pepper, paprika and herbs, and let boil down and thicken.

## Sauce Choron

This sauce is supposedly named after the Parisian chef Gustave Choron. In 1871 when Germans laid siege to the city and poverty was rampant, Choron was said to have served this sauce with stewed elephant trunks taken from animals at the Paris Zoo. Whether or not you believe this, the sauce is extremely delicious—even without the story!

*1 cup butter, 3 egg yolks, 1 tbs lemon juice,*
*Salt, Freshly ground pepper, 1–2 tbs tomato paste*

Melt butter over lowest possible heat until liquid. Over a hot double boiler, beat egg yolks, lemon juice, salt, pepper, tomato paste, and 3 tbs water until thick and creamy. Be careful not to boil or the egg will curdle! Gradually add melted butter, while stirring constantly. Serve sauce immediately with steak or fried fish fillets.

🍅 A quick version: Beat tomato paste into warm mayonnaise.

## Sauce all'Arrabbiata

This sauce gets its spiciness from the small, red chile peppers known in Italian as pepperoncini. It is mainly served with pasta.

*3½ oz streaky bacon, 1 lb plum tomatoes, 2 cloves garlic,*
*1 onion, 1 tbs butter, 2 red pepperoncini,*
*Salt, Freshly ground pepper, 1 tsp sugar*

Finely dice bacon. Blanch tomatoes, peel, cut into quarters, and remove cores. Purée tomatoes in a blender and then put through a fine strainer. Peel garlic and cut into paper-thin slices. Peel onion and dice finely.

In a pot, melt butter and brown diced bacon. Add garlic and onion and sauté briefly. Pour in strained tomatoes, add chile peppers, and simmer for 5 minutes. Then remove chile peppers. Spice up sauce with salt, pepper, and sugar.

## Tomato Tuna Sauce

*1¾ lb fully ripe tomatoes, 1 bunch green onions, 1 clove garlic,*
*1 tbs oil, 2 tbs sugar, Grated peel of 1 organic lemon,*
*2 tbs lemon juice, 2 cans tuna in water (about 5¼ oz), 2 tbs capers,*
*Salt, Freshly ground pepper, 1 tbs chopped Italian parsley*

Blanch tomatoes, peel, remove cores, and dice. Clean green onions and chop into fine rings. Peel garlic. Heat oil, roast garlic briefly, and remove again. Then squeeze garlic through a press and add to oil along with sugar. Once the sugar has melted, add tomatoes, lemon peel, and lemon juice. Simmer for 5 minutes. Drain tuna and shred. Stir tuna and capers into the sauce. Season with salt and pepper. Briefly bring to a boil and sprinkle with parsley. Serve with pasta or braised veal.

## Mexican Salsa for Tortilla Chips

Chips and salsa make an excellent south-of-the-border party appetizer or tasty snack with beer. Heat the tortilla chips in the oven and serve immediately with the salsa as dip.

*2¼ lb tomatoes, 7 oz onions, 2 cloves garlic, 1 fresh chile pepper,*
*2 tbs olive oil, 1 tsp finely crushed cumin seeds, 1 dash coriander,*
*1 tsp dried oregano, 1 tbs tomato paste, 2 tbs balsamic vinegar,*
*Salt, 1 tbs brown sugar, 1 tsp green peppercorns (and liquid),*
*Freshly ground black pepper*

Blanch tomatoes, peel, remove cores, and purée in a blender. Peel onions and garlic and mince. Slit open chile pepper, remove stem, seeds and interiors, and mince.

In a deep pan, heat olive oil. Add prepared vegetables, stir in cumin, coriander, oregano and tomato paste, and let boil down and thicken while stirring. Season to taste with vinegar, salt, sugar, and pepper to make it hot and spicy. Serve salsa warm.

🍅 Salsa keeps in the refrigerator for two days. Besides tortilla chips, it's delicious with cooked meat, poultry, and fish.

# PROVISIONS FROM THE
# FREEZER & CELLAR

Even in winter, there's no need to do without the popular love apple. You don't have to purchase the often bland winter tomatoes. There are many options for stretching out the summer tomato season by preserving the tomatoes in a variety of ways. For example, they can be canned, dried, or frozen.

Canning used to require canning jars, rubber rings, and canning pots. Do you remember how sometimes the jars would still take on air after canning and all that hard work would be wasted? Nowadays, you can use practical screw-top jars.

For a long time and until only a few years ago, drying tomatoes was a done by only die-hard gourmets, the backpacker crowd, and, of course, Italians. And we were very hesitant to freeze them. But it isn't such a difficult enterprise, really. You can freeze the flesh without the seeds, freeze the juice, or even freeze whole tomatoes (with or without the peel). Frozen tomatoes are suitable for soups, sauces, casseroles, and pizzas. Tomatoes can also be frozen in finished dishes, including soups and sauces. To cut the amount of work in half, make double batches. Don't thaw frozen tomatoes or they become mushy and lose too much juice. Always use them unthawed.

Many fresh dishes require only the tomato flesh. But don't throw away the juice and seeds. Freeze them in batches and use them in winter soups, meat sauces, or fish dishes.

# Dried Tomatoes

Tomatoes dried on walls or in drying ovens under the southern sun of Italy or Spain have a more intense flavor because 94% of the moisture is extracted. However, they do not retain all their nutritional content. They're available for purchase in plastic containers, marinated in oil and herbs, or salted in foil packs. If you buy dried tomatoes, taste them before processing. If they're very salty, you need to soak them and, if necessary, change the water several times. If you buy them in oil, you'll want to reduce the amount of fat you add to the recipe.

Dried tomatoes require more liquid than fresh, so use more liquid when making soups and sauces. About 7 oz dried tomatoes correspond to 12 oz fresh. Finely chopped, they're especially delicious in salads, soups, and sauces.

At latitudes farther north than Spain and Italy (say, Boston or Seattle), tomatoes aren't dried in the sun but in the oven as described below.

*9 lb ripe plum tomatoes, 2 tsp salt,*
*Fresh chopped herbs (e.g., basil, thyme, or oregano; optional)*

Cut tomatoes in half lengthwise and remove cores. If desired, combine herbs with the salt. Preheat the oven to 250°F. Place tomatoes on a drying rack (or oven rack) with the cut sides up, sprinkle with (herb) salt, and dry in the oven for 4 hours, leaving the oven door cracked open. Then turn tomatoes and dry for another 4 hours. Then test the tomatoes: They must be dry but still pliable. If you dry them too long, they'll be tough. If you don't dry them long enough, they'll mold. Because different tomatoes have different drying times, you may have to leave them in the oven longer.

You can reduce the drying time by removing the seeds after you cut open the tomatoes and drying only the flesh (2–2½ hours per side). Place dried tomatoes in small linen bags and store in a cool, well ventilated place (preferably a cellar).

## Dried Tomatoes in Oil

*1 cup Dried Tomatoes (recipe on page 104), 2 cloves garlic,*
*1 tbs pickled green peppercorns (or 2 dried chile peppers),*
*About 2 cups cold-pressed olive oil*

Peel and chop garlic. Layer tomatoes, garlic, green peppercorns, or chile peppers (cut in half) in a large screw-top jar. Add oil to about ¼ inch above the tomatoes. Seal and store in a cool, dark place.

🍅 If desired, add 1 bay leaf or sliced black olives.

## Tomato Purée

Once you open the jar or thaw it out, purée keeps in the refrigerator for several days. Because of its high concentration, use it only sparingly in stews, soups, stocks, and sauces.

*4½ lb ripe, meaty tomatoes, Salt, Freshly ground pepper*

Cut tomatoes in half, remove cores, and bring to a boil without water. Simmer for 20 minutes, stir, and simmer for another 20 minutes. Put through a strainer. Season purée with salt and pepper and return to a boil. If the mixture is too runny, reduce it further. When it has the consistency of paste, pour it immediately into hot, sterilized jelly jars and seal. Or let cool and freeze in individual containers.

## Danish Tomato Purée

*2 stalks celery, 2 onions, 2¼ lb beefsteak tomatoes,*
*3 stalks oregano, 1½ tsp salt, 5 black peppercorns, ¼–½ tsp sugar*

Clean celery and chop finely. Peel and dice onions. Cut tomatoes in half and remove cores. Rinse oregano. In a saucepan, combine vegetables, oregano, salt, pepper and sugar, and cover and simmer for 1 hour. Then put the mixture through a strainer, return to the pot, and bring to a boil without covering. Season to taste and pour immediately into hot, sterilized jelly jars, and seal or freeze in individual containers.

## Ketchup

At the beginning of the 18th century, English sailors brought "kichop" home from Malaysia. It was a sauce made from oysters, mushrooms, and nuts. From England, it was exported to the U.S. where the idea of thickening the sauce with tomatoes was born. In 1869 when the American, Henry J. Heinz, began large-scale marketing of this tomato sauce as ketchup, the name took hold worldwide.

*4½ lb fully ripe plum tomatoes, 2 onions,*
*4 tbs red wine vinegar or balsamic vinegar, 1 tbs salt,*
*2 tbs brown sugar (or ¼ cup honey), Freshly ground pepper, Tabasco sauce*

Cut tomatoes into quarters and remove seeds. Peel onions and cut into quarters. In a saucepan, simmer onions and tomatoes without water for 20 minutes. Put through a fine-mesh strainer. Season purée with vinegar, salt, sugar or honey, pepper and Tabasco, and gently simmer uncovered while stirring until you have a thick paste. Cooking time is 60-75 minutes and depends on the juice content of the tomatoes. But be careful—the purée burns easily! Immediately after cooking, transfer to hot, sterilized jelly jars or bottles, and seal tightly. Ketchup keeps for about 6 months. Once you open a jar or bottle, it needs to be refrigerated.

## Spiced Ketchup

*1 recipe Ketchup (see page 106), 1 red bell pepper, 1 chile pepper,*
*½ tsp each of ground cloves, mace, allspice, and ginger,*
*1 tsp mustard seeds, 1 tsp white peppercorns,*
*½ tbs each of chopped herbs, as desired (e.g., borage, basil,*
*savory, purslane, salad burnet, hyssop)*

Cut bell and chile peppers in half, remove stems, seeds and interiors, and cook with tomatoes and onions as described in the ketchup recipe. Put through a strainer and season with cloves, mace, allspice, and ginger.

Place mustard seeds and peppercorns, and any herbs in a tea filter bag, tie shut, and suspend in the paste. Cook as described, then remove the bag and squeeze it out thoroughly. Transfer spiced ketchup to hot, sterilized jelly jars, and seal tightly.

🍅 Mix 3½ oz raisins, 1 chopped garlic clove, and a ¾-inch piece of cleaned horseradish into the raw vegetables and cook.

## Danish Apple Ketchup

*2¼ lb tomatoes, 10½ oz tart apples,*
*2 onions, 1 tbs salt, 1 tbs honey*

Blanch tomatoes, peel, cut into quarters, and remove cores. Peel apples, cut into quarters, and remove cores. Peel onions and cut in half. Purée all 3 in a blender.

Pour mixture into a pot and simmer uncovered along with salt and honey for 1 hour. Stir frequently. Transfer immediately to hot, sterilized jelly jars, and seal. Or let cool and freeze in batches.

🍅 Try this ketchup with apricots and apples (3½ oz dried apricots, 7 oz apples).

## Moni's Chutney

*4½ lb tomatoes, 1 lb onions, 1 lb sugar, 3½ tbs salt,*
*1 tbs freshly grated horseradish, 1 tsp each of cayenne pepper,*
*Hungarian hot paprika, ginger, and allspice,*
*½ tsp cloves, 1 cup wine vinegar*

Blanch tomatoes, peel, remove cores, and chop coarsely. Peel and dice onions. In a saucepan, simmer tomatoes and onions for 30 minutes. Add sugar, salt, horseradish, and spices. Pour in vinegar, stir, and simmer uncovered for another 2 hours while stirring. Transfer immediately to hot, sterilized jelly jars, seal tightly, and let cool. Stored in a cool place, chutney keeps for 2–3 months.

## Tomato Chutney

Stored in a cool place, this chutney keeps for about two months. It's delicious with steak and roasts, can be used to season sauces and, when mixed with yogurt, makes a wonderful dip.

*4½ lb tomatoes, 1 cup apple cider vinegar, 2⅔ cups sugar,*
*1 pinch salt, 1 tsp allspice berries, 1 tsp whole cloves,*
*1 stick cinnamon, 3½ oz raisins, 2½ oz chopped pine nuts or almonds*

On the previous day, blanch tomatoes, peel, cut into quarters, and remove cores. Transfer to a bowl, pour ½ cup apple cider vinegar on top and marinate for 12 hours.

On the next day, bring remaining vinegar to a boil with sugar until the sugar has dissolved. Add salt. Place allspice, cloves, and cinnamon in a tea filter bag and tie it shut. In a large pot, combine tomatoes, raisins, pine nuts or almonds, and spice bag and pour in the sugar–vinegar mixture. Simmer for 30 minutes while stirring. If the tomatoes have not yet disintegrated, mash them thoroughly and return the purée to a boil. Transfer immediately to hot, sterilized jelly jars, seal tightly, and let cool.

🍅 Cook 1 lb peeled, diced apples or the corn stripped from 2 ears along with the tomatoes.

## Tomato Relish

*2 plum-sized pieces of pickled ginger (from a jar),*
*1 organic lime, 1 lb cherry tomatoes, ½ cup brown sugar,*
*7 tbs white wine vinegar, 1 tsp salt*

Finely chop ginger. Dice lime with the peel. In a pot, combine tomatoes and all the other ingredients, bring to a boil, and stir until the sugar is dissolved. Then simmer for 45 minutes, stirring occasionally. When the cooking time is over, transfer immediately to hot, sterilized jelly jars, and seal tightly.

## American Relish

*14 dried tomatoes in oil, 12 shallots, 1 lb cherry tomatoes,*
*3 tbs oil from the dried tomatoes, 4 tbs apricot jam, 1 dash sugar*

Drain dried tomatoes and dice finely. Peel shallots and dice finely. Blanch cherry tomatoes, peel, cut in half, and remove seeds.

In a pot, heat oil and sweat shallots. Add dried tomatoes and braise over low heat for 10 minutes. Add tomatoes and simmer until tender. Then stir in apricot jam and season relish to taste with sugar. Simmer for about 1 minute more. Then let cool and serve or transfer immediately to hot, sterilized jelly jars, and seal tightly.

## Canned Tomatoes

*3⅓ lb ripe cherry tomatoes, 1¾ cups onions (about 14 oz),*
*4 cloves garlic, 1 tbs black peppercorns, 4 stalks tarragon,*
*4 bay leaves, 2 cups white wine vinegar,*
*2 cups white wine, 1 tbs salt, 1 tbs sugar*

Cut a wedge out of cherry tomatoes to remove cores. Peel onions and cut into rings. Peel garlic and cut in half lengthwise. Layer tomatoes, onions, and garlic in four 24 oz jelly jars, sprinkling peppercorns between layers. Rinse tarragon and top each jar with 1 stalk tarragon and 1 bay leaf. Combine vinegar, wine, salt, and sugar, bring to a boil and simmer for 10–15 minutes. Pour boiling liquid over the tomatoes and seal jars immediately. Let marinate for at least 3–4 days before consuming. Store in a cool place.

## Ginger Tomatoes

This recipe uses green tomatoes—not unripe red tomatoes but the variety cultivated to be green.

*2¼ lb ripe green tomatoes, 1 tbs vinegar water (1 part vinegar, 2 parts water),*
*2 large pieces dried ginger, 3-4 whole cloves, 1 tbs black peppercorns,*
*1 stick cinnamon, Peel of 1 organic lemon, 3⅓ cups sugar, 3 cups mild vinegar*

Pierce the tomatoes several times with a toothpick. Bring vinegar water to a boil, add tomatoes, return to a boil, and then let cool. Discard water. Place ginger, cloves, peppercorns, cinnamon, and lemon peel in a tea filter bag and tie it shut. Place tomatoes and spice bag in a pot. Combine sugar and vinegar, boil until the sugar has dissolved, and pour over tomatoes. Simmer for 5–10 minutes, then remove spice bag. Layer tomatoes in hot, sterilized jelly jars, and pour the boiling-hot liquid over the top. Seal tightly.

If desired, place bay leaves, dried Spanish peppers, and 1 tbs dill seeds between the tomato layers.

## Spicy Tomato Preserves

These preserves can be used to spice up game sauces or served with meat dishes or cheese. They're also delicious on ciabatta or French country bread.

*2¼ lb ripe beefsteak tomatoes, 2 red onions,*
*4 fresh chile peppers, ¼ cup fresh lemon juice, ½ tsp butter (optional),*
*1 box fruit pectin (about 2 oz), 4½ cups sugar, measured into separate bowl*

Blanch tomatoes, peel, remove cores, and dice finely. Peel onions and cut into small cubes. Cut chile peppers in half, remove stems, seeds and interiors, and chop finely. Place in saucepan. Bring to a boil. Reduce heat to low; cover and simmer 10 minutes, stirring occasionally. Measure exactly 3 cups prepared fruit into 6- or 8- quart saucepot. Add lemon juice. Stir pectin into tomato mixture in saucepot. Add butter to reduce foaming, if desired. Bring mixture to full rolling boil on high heat, stirring constantly. Stir in sugar. Return to full rolling boil and boil exactly 1 minute, stirring constantly. Remove from heat. Skim off any foam with a metal spoon. Transfer immediately to hot, sterilized jelly jars, and seal.

For seedless preserves, use only the tomato flesh. Weigh it and adapt the amount of sugar so you have a 1-to-1 ratio.

## Tomato Jam

*6⅔ lb ripe tomatoes, 1¾ cups sugar and 1 cinnamon stick per 2¼ lb purée*

Cut up tomatoes and cook without water until flesh disintegrates. Put through a strainer and weigh the purée. Add the correct amount of sugar and cinnamon and simmer until all the water is gone. Remove cinnamon. Transfer immediately to hot, sterilized jelly jars, seal tightly, and stand upside-down for several minutes.

For a modern tomato jam, simply combine tomatoes, sugar in a 1-to-1 ratio, lemon juice, and pectin according to package directions and season with cinnamon sticks or vanilla beans.

Try this recipe using green tomatoes and a finely chopped apple or with 1 cup plums or squash.

# BEVERAGES

Besides being refreshing, beverages prepared with tomato juice are also nutritious and satisfying. If you drink them before a meal or as an appetite suppressant in between, they'll take the edge off your hunger.

When making beverages with milk or yogurt, always whisk the juice into the milk and not the other way around, because the acid in the tomatoes tends to curdle the milk.

## Spiced Tomato Juice

*1 cup tomato juice (prepackaged), 1 pinch herb salt, Freshly ground black pepper,*
*2–3 dashes Tabasco or Worcestershire sauce, Several ice cubes (optional)*

Whisk together tomato juice, herb salt, pepper and seasoning sauce, and season liberally to taste. In summer, serve with ice cubes and in winter, just well chilled. A little vitamin boost!

## Tomato Milk

*Makes 2–3 tall glasses:*
*2–3 juicy tomatoes, 1 tbs lemon juice,*
*Celery salt, Lemon pepper, 1 cup milk (or yogurt stirred until creamy),*
*Organic lemon peel for garnish (or mint leaves)*

Blanch tomatoes, peel, and remove seeds, setting aside the juice. Remove cores and dice finely. Put juice through a strainer and season with lemon juice, celery salt, and lemon pepper.

Briefly whisk milk or yogurt. Pour juice into milk while stirring. Place several cubes of tomato in a glass and pour milk over the top. Serve immediately—if the drink stands too long, it can separate. Garnish with a spiral of lemon peel or with mint leaves.

## Tomato Flip

Flips are beverages with egg yolk whisked into them. This makes them ideal as the "hair of the dog" the morning after a party.

*Makes 1 glass:*
*1 egg yolk, 8 tsp ketchup (recipe on page 106), 4 tsp gin,*
*1 pinch freshly ground black pepper, 1 pinch sugar, Freshly grated nutmeg*

In a cocktail shaker, combine ketchup, gin, pepper and sugar, and shake vigorously, pour into a tall glass, and dust with nutmeg. Serve with a straw.

If you want the flip to be ice-cold, place 2–3 ice cubes in the glass before pouring in the flip.

## Bloody Mary

When prepared with gin instead of vodka, this classic is simply called a Tomato Cocktail. Without alcohol, it's a Virgin Mary.

*Makes 1 glass:*
*10 tsp tomato juice, 2 dashes Worcestershire sauce,*
*2 drops lemon juice, Celery salt, Freshly ground white pepper,*
*2 dashes Tabasco sauce, 4 tsp gin*

In a blender, combine tomato juice, Worcestershire sauce, lemon juice, celery salt, pepper, Tabasco and gin, and blend. Pour into a glass and drink well chilled.

## Special

*Makes 1 glass:*
*2–3 ice cubes, 1 tbs lemon juice, 2 tsp tomato juice,*
*4 tsp brandy, 3 dashes Worcestershire sauce, 3 dashes Tabasco sauce,*
*1 pinch salt, Soda water, Freshly ground black pepper*

Place ice cubes in a tall glass. Combine lemon juice, tomato juice, brandy, seasoning sauces and salt, and whisk thoroughly. Add soda water. Pour over the ice cubes and sprinkle with pepper.

## Tomato Punch

Served in winter, this punch will warm you from within—for example, after a long walk.

*Makes 4 glasses:*
*8 tsp freshly squeezed orange juice, 2 cups red wine, ½ cup tomato juice (prepackaged),*
*1 pinch salt, 1 pinch sugar, 4 tsp Cointreau, 1 orange slice for garnish*

Heat orange juice, red wine and tomato juice (do not boil), and season with salt and sugar. Just before serving, add Cointreau. Pour very hot into tall mulled wine glasses. Garnish with an orange slice.

 If you want to make the punch "Christmassy," briefly suspend a bag of mulled wine spices in the pot.

 You can also serve this punch in the summer well chilled.

# LIST OF RECIPES

## Appetizers & Salads

## Soups & Stews

## Salads & Sides

## Pizzas & Hearty Tortes

## Vegetable Dishes & Casseroles

## Meat Dishes

## Fish & Seafood Dishes

## Dips & Sauces

## Provisions from the Freezer & Cellar

## Beverages